This book is f

> This book which is an account of the Author's extraordinary life experiences travelling through childhood, teenage years, marriage, domestic violence, resulting in the agony of being forced to leave her children and divorce, this story is at times shocking, touching and thought provoking while at the same time written with humour and positivity.

> Through these experiences the Author shares knowledge, understanding and experience in a masterful book that can enrich readers' lives in many ways.

> The Author's willingness to be candid and vulnerable throughout allows for a beautifully relatable journey.

> The book is about survival and strength. How the Author survived all that she went through and came out smiling, is nothing short of a miracle.

> You will be drawn in immediately. This book is at times deeply moving with heart breaking decisions the Author had to endure but you will find inspiration and strength on every page.

> A riveting read this is a book you won't want to put down.

What people are saying

A riveting read- this is a book you won't want to put down. The author's account of her extraordinary life experiences is at times shocking, touching and thought provoking while at the same time written with humour and positivity. She is likeable, relatable and as a reader you are willing her fortunes to change. From start to finish Ruth's encounters will keep you enthralled.

Claire Darling

A thorough and thought-provoking page-turner. The book is very well written and flows really well and is easy to read. I like that the author knows just the right amount of descriptions to give all the characters, whilst giving a depth of understanding of their personality and their motives. It was heart breaking and painful at times, but I like the underlying humour and strength and the message it portrays of leaning to survive, love and laugh. The author's willingness to be candid and vulnerable throughout allows for a beautifully relatable journey. She shares knowledge, understanding and experience in a masterful book that can enrich readers' lives in many ways. Don't pass this book by; it's well-worth your time.

Peter Hodgson

I was privileged to be one of the first people to read the whole manuscript. Having shared some of the unhappiness and trauma the author went through at the time, it was still a compulsive read for me. The author expresses herself and her emotions very simply yet passionately and the reader can easily identify with her pain. How she survived all that she went through and came out smiling, is nothing short of a miracle. A must-read. And then there is the sequels!

Jilly-Anne Powell

I was drawn in immediately. To Love Honour and Betray is at times deeply moving with heart breaking decisions the Author had to endure . I feel privileged to be one of the first to read it and looking forward to the next book.

Margaret Gowans

About the author...

Ruth Tunnicliffe is a mum of three and has lived quite an eventful life, and by putting pen to paper this work of pure liberation will be sure to help other women treading similar paths of enforced agreeability.

A fault in society is that women are effectively conditioned to please others, to not shout too loud and not to complain. And Ruth's life which is documented so beautifully in To Love, Honour and Betray is a demonstration of how 'putting up and shutting up' can result in the most catastrophic and bizarre situations.

Ruth said: "I always wanted to make people happy, and doing something that would make someone unhappy, even if it was for the best was unthinkable and the worst thing ever. I am a people pleaser."

Ruth predominantly wrote the book as a way to explain her life to her three children, her eldest boy and girl she was forced to leave behind in an urgent police-backed escape from her abusive first husband.

She said: "I was never frightened or worried about leaving the children with him because that's all he really wanted. As soon as I had given birth to those kids he wanted rid of me, he wasn't interested in me but I was convinced that he would never harm them. He had told me over the 10 years we were together that they were his kids and I could never take them from him. After that long, I believed him. I knew I could never leave them so just kept on hoping that things would get better and I never planned to leave them with him. I knew that he would have harmed himself if I'd taken them from him and I knew that much 100% so I couldn't do that. It would be me who had to make the ultimate sacrifice eventually, not him".

After so many unusual situations and events had happened to Ruth people said to her 'you need to write a book' so she thought she would start writing things down. Ruth began writing in 2011. It started off as a cathartic thing. Basically just to get all these incidents out of her head and on paper in the hope that it would help her come to terms with her difficult decisions. With leaving the kids she could never get over it. She emotionally couldn't let it go. It broke her.

She said "I was constantly grieving for them".
"I was living with that guilt and eating myself up constantly, it was just driving me mad. I had tried counselling and it didn't work for me. It just made me cry and feel even more guilty."

Ruth had always said that she needed at least 3 months to finish writing the book and get it all done. She was unable to keep picking it up and putting down in between her "day job" as a legal secretary. Then came lockdown 1.

Ruth had been made redundant so after she had decorated the house she decided that she should pick up the book and try and finish it, even if she just printed it off and gave it to the three kids, that's the most important thing to her.' So Ruth made herself finish it."

She said "Once I started to write I couldn't stop. I had a friend reading each chapter. She is brutally honest and I knew I could trust her tell me the truth about my writing style and the contents, she loved it. I would write as many chapters as I could during the day and then send her the chapters at night for her to read. Every chapter I sent was helping me unravel my life. Although very difficult at times, I sometimes struggled to go back to certain places and situations in my head but with the help of my friend I kept going. She couldn't get enough of it, and was always waiting for the next chapter. She told me it was so easy to read and it flowed really well."

In Ruth's life story a second marriage followed, a marriage which Ruth almost drifted into, not wanting to disappoint a man who clearly liked her a lot more than she liked him. But this man became more and more paranoid, frightening and near-forced Ruth to go to live in Cornwall, taking her even further away from her children in Yorkshire so that she could care for his aging father and he could claim the inheritance.

The situation came to a head years later when Ruth, her second son, and daughter who by that time was living with her, were forced to go into hiding when he began stalking them and behaving erratically and dangerously.

After both of these marriages Ruth set about cheerfully building back her life, she always managed to keep her sense of fun and humour, but faced prejudice from friends and acquaintances who naturally thought they would have done things differently.

Ruth said: "In my first marriage their dad got away with mistreating me mentally and physically and showed no remorse. He made sure that everyone was pitying him and he was going around getting sympathy, I was left ashamed and guilt ridden because I let him treat me like that. I couldn't believe that someone who was supposed to love me would do that to me, I couldn't admit that to myself. Also because he was my children's dad I respected him for that but found it hard to accept that my children's father would behave like that towards me."

But what the book shows is how these things can and do happen so naturally, that before you know it you are in a perilous situation! There is also a lot of humour in the book, and Ruth is not afraid to laugh at herself, and focus of the humour in a situation.

She said: "Some of my story is funny, especially relating to my daughter, she could always see the funny side even in the worst of predicaments! There is a bit in the book where we are in hiding from my second husband and racing around putting all our stuff in bin bags, when I receive a call from a social worker to say that they have found a place for us in a hostel. "I turned to tell the kids and my daughter immediately says 'HOSTEL I'm sorry?! Don't you mean a hotel?!" And we all fell about laughing! She can just make anything funny within an instant!

"We did have some fun, I have had a lot of fun in my life it hasn't all been misery and I hope that comes across in the book. There are several incidents that still made me laugh out loud when I wrote them down"

It is safe to say that Ruth's story is a page-turner, a book you read in one on two sitting and can't put down. Written as Ruth speaks, reading the book is like sitting down with a friend as they tell you the best 'real life' stories ever. But it has also served as a very cathartic and healing process for Ruth, who has been through so much, and rebuilt her life more times than most people will ever have to.

As a final thought she added: "When I finished the book I just thought 'That's it, I'm almost clean again' It sounds really cheesy but that's how it felt. Each chapter I was getting rid of all the upset, all the guilt.

"My life has been riddled with guilt from the minute I left the kids and my decisions since then seem to be down to that, I feel like I have now released myself from the guilt and know me now. More than I ever did before. I am now 150% me, I do care about other people and will put their needs and feeling above my own, it's in my nature, but now I have put everything in its right place. All my ducks are in a row and I can relax now."

Acknowledgements

Rachel Marie Gowans,
Claire Darling,
Jilly-Anne Powell,
Margaret Gowans,
Susan Mears,
Janet Lee Chapman,
Hayley Anne Finch
and Peter Hodgson.

Thank you!

Dedication

In Memory of my lovely
Mother and Father,
my much loved
Brother and Sister
and everyone who has
encouraged me to do this.

*The point when you realise
something is very wrong*

To Love,
Honour,
and Betray

Ruth Tunnicliffe

Published by
Filament Publishing Ltd
16, Croydon Road, Beddington
Croydon, Surrey CR0 4PA
www.filamentpublishing.com
+44(0)20 8688 2598

To Love, Honour, and Betray
Ruth Tunnicliffe
ISBN 978-1-913623-63-0
© 2021 Ruth Tunnicliffe

Printed in the UK

Table of Contents

PROLOGUE

I crept into the bedroom as quietly as I could, when Tyler, my son, suddenly sat bolt upright in his bunk bed, his face beaming, he turned to look at me, saying with delight, "Mum, you're back."

The overwhelming feeling of panic seemed to start in my toes and travel through my bloodstream.

As my whole body froze, I looked at his beautiful, bright face. I was almost choking, when I started stuttering "No... no... I'm not ... I can't ...."

I burst into floods of tears. Shaking from head to foot, I just didn't know which way to turn.

I panicked, dropped everything I was carrying, as I turned to run along the landing. Not daring to stop and look into Sarah's room, I swept past my daughter's bedroom door. I could hear Tyler crying. I kept running. It was unbearable and I felt desperate, in a complete state of panic, as huge sadness stole my breath away, I was totally overwhelmed.

I just kept on running down the stairs, with my head down, sobbing uncontrollably, mumbling to myself, "No... no...I can't do this" I pushed past the policeman who was guarding the lounge door, in an attempt to stop Donovan, my ex-husband, from getting to me, who was now glaring in my direction.

He was standing in the doorway, with tears in his eyes but there was a hidden anger behind those eyes. A sinister expression, it terrified me. I just had to get away from him. I had no choice.

As I stumbled over the front doorstep and collapsed into the back of the police car, crying inconsolably, my stomach churning, I realised that was the moment I'd feared the most. I had no choice now, I had to leave my home and children forever. I couldn't go back there.
Fighting back her tears, my friend, Rita said, "It's okay, I will get your stuff."

She went back into the house to find the clothes I'd dropped as I bolted out of the house. She scooped up as many items as she could, putting them into black binbags. Sitting there in the car, watching her, the emotional train hit me like a ton of bricks, as I knew then that I was losing my children, I would never again be with them fulltime. My never-ending journey of sadness, grief and guilt had only just begun. On that day my heart completely shattered into what felt like million pieces. My boy, Tyler, was seven, and my little girl, Sarah, was just four.

What the hell was I going to do without them both?

Part One

Little Sophia

Chapter One

Happy Families 1960

I was sitting on the back seat of my dad's car, wedged in between my siblings, Harry and Dina. I turned to say a silent goodbye to the village sign, that I had sat on it many times in the past. We were moving to a new home. I wondered what lay ahead for me. I was 11 years old, a skinny, quiet, shy and almost timid child. It was a sad day. We had lived in one of only two Council houses in a very small village. We had an amazing view of the moors out of our back windows. There was a large field just to the right of our house, it had a great big tree, right slap bang in the middle of it.

I don't have many childhood memories, though this one stuck with me. I was happily playing out in front of the house on what bit of grass we had when, suddenly, I became aware that there was something above me. I looked straight up into the sky, as this bloody, great, big, red glider was about to crash down in the field, just missing the huge tree. I absolutely freaked out; I will never forget that image. It was like a great big bird swooping down on me. My whole body shook when I looked up. I must have been about 5 years old. My Mum told me that I bolted into the house, screaming my head off, I was absolutely terrified. I flatly refused to leave the house for the next few days, no matter how hard she tried to coax me outside. Luckily, nobody had been killed and the pilot had just stepped out and walked away.

After a couple of days, a lorry turned up with a load of blokes, who dismantled the glider and took it away. My Mum managed to get me outside eventually. She stood with me as we watched the men dismantle it. She was trying to prove to me that this machine was not going to hurt me, there was nothing to fear. Already, it was too late for that, the near miss image was imprinted in my head. Seeing such a huge object above me just outside the house had given me quite a shock. For years and, even to this day, if any gliders, small planes, helicopters, drones or anything in flight, should creep up on me, I can't help but immediately put my head down and find it difficult to look at it. For years, airports were an absolutely 'no go' zone for me!

Going back a couple of years, the other early childhood memory I have from around three years old, was when I contracted septic arthritis in my right hip. It didn't hurt, my right leg had gone zigzag-shaped from my hip to my knee. It happened completely out of the blue literally overnight. I remember being taken to hospital in an old, cream coloured, ambulance, like those on the tv show, *Heartbeat*. The condition seemed to have hit me with no warning, I was told that I had fallen the day before it developed bang slap onto a toy tin drum and my leg became bent from my hip down to my knee. That sounds weird to me, I didn't see how a tin drum could do such damage, but I spent weeks in Hospital with my leg tied by traction to the bottom of the bed. A lovely Staff Nurse would carry me around the wards, occasionally, to visit other children, as I was unable to walk on my own. I liked her, she had a big bun right on the top of her head and she was really pretty. She had big eyelashes and smelt lovely. One day I overhead the doctors say that it may come back to me when I was 7 years old and, later, there was a risk it may come back in 7-year cycles. This gave me a secret silent dread of that age. Funny how things stay with you. Thank God it never did come back. I was left with a wonky back and my right shoulder sticks out a bit more than my left one … must be something to do with the traction, who knows?

I used to spend a lot of my time with my best friend, Lizzie. She lived at the farm across the road from us, with her Mum, Auntie Alicia, Dad, Uncle David, and her brother, Rex. Of course, they became my adopted Auntie and Uncle, we were not related. Lizzie was the same age as me, we were in the same class at the really small primary school in the village. My Mum was a dinner lady there sometimes. I remember the puddings from school, one of them was gorgeous vanilla sponge cut into great big chunks with peaches and hot custard, I loved it. My Mum would always give me a big portion. Sometimes there was a similar cake type thing, but they ruined it by putting jam and coconut on the top of it. Hate coconut! Anyway, I always remember Auntie Alicia used to put those bits of ripped up sheets in Lizzie's super thin hair overnight to create some sort of ringlets. Lizzie had really pale, doll like, skin, long eyelashes and big brown eyes. I used to think her family were really posh, as they had loads of rooms in their farmhouse, some of which were spare rooms, and they were always really tidy, with twin beds in them, a bit like a hotel room. In contrast, the rooms in our house were never empty, they were stacked full of our rubbish.

At Lizzie's house, they had little, light blue, telephones with white wires in each bedroom and we would talk to each other from each room, as if we were in a posh hotel pretending to order room service. Their house seemed enormous to my child's eyes, though I am sure it wasn't, everything just seemed to be so big then. Auntie Alicia was striking to look at, she always wore bright red lipstick and with her shoulder length, jet black, wavy hair and her dark brown eyes, she looked like a beautiful star out of an old film. I liked her a lot, I think she like me, too. She had a beautiful face and smile, she used to hug me a lot and I sniff her lovely perfume.

Often Lizzie and I would make up shows and plays. We would send invitations and present our shows to my Mum and Auntie Alicia in Lizzie's large, country kitchen. She had a large, wooden, blanket box, full of big hats with feathers on, and silk dresses of all different colours. I imagine Auntie Alicia used to wear them to go to the hunt balls, and such like occasions, to do with the farming community. There was one dress that was strapless and slim fitted, with netting gathered across the boobs, it was lilac and pink coloured, long and floaty. It was my favourite dress, I used to make a bee line for that dress, I would put it on and prance around the garden in it, with white stiletto heels, and dump a great, big, floppy sun hat on my head. I used to feel so special in that dress. Just like a film star.

The farm was crammed with dairy cows, mostly, though there were some pigs, too, and some empty pigsties on the farm. I remember my dad used to laugh at the pigs. They tickled him every time he saw them. It was good to see him belly laughing. That didn't happen often. We would turn the pig sties into little houses and invite each other round for afternoon tea, made up of mud pies and bits of grass for salad! I think we were allowed to do that, as we had to swill and clean them out first. Nice one, Uncle

David! It saved him a job and it kept us out of mischief, too. We would spend ages scrubbing the floors and in the summer months they would dry instantly. We used to make flower arrangements in jam jars from wildflowers in the fields and put them in the windows of our "homes". We made perfume out of rose petals, too. We loved home building; we'd spent hours upon hours in our houses. Once, my dad made us a go cart, we called it a bogey. It was made up of old pram wheels, with a couple of planks fixed between them, and some string to help steer it. We'd all pile on it and go hurtling down the village. It was such fun, though, looking back, very dangerous. We were fearless. Such happy times.

When Uncle David harvested the corn, we would shimmy up and down the ladder on the side of the big, round, tin containers and we would get inside them, jumping around in the corn, as we sank into it. Afterwards, our shoes would be full of corn. I can still feel that between my toes. Such vivid memories. Blimey, that was risky, looking back, what if we'd got stuck and we could've drowned in that corn! If Uncle David knew we had done that, we would have been in deep trouble. He was a very calm and quiet man most of the time, but I reckon he had a proper Yorkshire temper when he blew.

I was always at the farm after school and in the school holidays, Lizzie never seemed to come over to my house, unless it was a birthday or something, I never knew why. Maybe our house was boring. We always had proper lemonade with ice cubes in proper little glasses at Lizzie's house, I would make it last as long as I could, sipping it slowly until it had gone flat. Pretending it was a gin and tonic! That was proper Lemonade not the sour, old crap that we had, made with a soda stream, that stuff went flat before you even had time to drink it. One day, I came hurtling down the village road on my bike, behind my older sister, Dina, on hers, when she stopped suddenly, without giving me any notice. I went straight into the back of her and flew over the handlebars, landing on my nose, which burst, there was blood everywhere, it was awful. I was swallowing all the blood down the back of my throat. I am not sure why, but my Mum wasn't at home, she must have been at work. When Auntie Alicia heard me screaming, she rushed out to see what all the fuss was about, scooped me up and took me into her house to patch me up. My nose wouldn't stop bleeding, she had to stuff my nostrils with cotton wool, the blood still pouring down the back of my throat, as it wouldn't seem to stop. I was laying on the sofa in the kitchen, being given that lovely lemonade to help get rid of the taste of blood. It was almost worth having the accident, just for another glass of that wonderful lemonade. I had a terrible headache though and that taste of dry blood just wouldn't go away.

Uncle David had an old Wolseley car he kept in a separate garage at the side of the farmhouse, it was a deep maroon colour, with cream leather interior and it was very shiny. They only took it out on a Sunday to go off to Northallerton to see their family. We weren't allowed in the garage, but we would sneak in and sit in the car. It was always unlocked. I went in it a couple of times, I noticed the smell of leather was strong, I thought that it must have felt so special being allowed to travel in such style. My family always had old bangers that kept breaking down and were too small to fit us all in comfortably, I was always wedged in the middle of Dina and my older brother Harry, I could hardly move. I would watch Lizzie go off in her Sunday best clothes and curled hair in the morning, and I'd just mooch about all day sitting on the village sign playing with the bobbles on the sign, waiting for them to come back, so I could go and play with her again. Sometimes I'd wait all day for her, only to be told that she was too tired, she had to go in for her bath, and no doubt to start putting those weird strips of sheets in her hair to nail on the curls. How Victorian!

We would go down to the local beck, next to the church. There was a spooky wood next to the church, we named it thunder wood after we got caught playing in there once and a really frightening thunderstorm came out of nowhere. The thunder and lightning scared the life out of us, though the rain never used to bother us, we used to play out in all weathers, get completely soaked and then, we would drip dry, we were tough and never seemed to get colds or anything else. Even when we had a sniffle, we were told to get outside in the fresh air. We never played indoors, unless it was dark outside. We used to march off, armed with our buckets, to catch bull heads and little tiddlers. On the way home, we would go to the Post Office for a bag of penny chews, or a sherbet dib dab. The Post Office was run by what seemed like a very old man. I am sure he was not that old, though everyone looked old to me when I was that age. He was very tall, used to wear an old worn-out suit with a waistcoat, he had bright blue eyes and grey stubble on his big chin. He had a very friendly face with round glasses and a pipe sticking out of his mouth all the time. We used to send him upstairs to get tobacco for our dad, so that we could pinch sweets from behind the counter whilst he was gone. He must have been bad on his feet, because he took so long to get the tobacco, that we had actually had time to weigh out a quarter of sherbet lemons and put them neatly into a small paper bag. Why we had to have exactly a quarter I don't know! It must have been the thrill of using the scales. It was ridiculous to think he was willingly or able to sell tobacco to us, we were so under the legal age.

On Sundays, the ice-cream van would come at 3pm, parking up outside the village primary school. The ice cream was world-famous. It was the highlight of our week! I looked forward to it, I always got a small tub. It was gorgeous, I used to stir mine with that little plastic spoon until it went all creamy. For some reason, though, my dad used to get that cross, scary face on, and tell me off for doing that. He would bark at me to eat it properly. I enjoyed it much better that way, I eventually used to hide it from my dad behind his chair, hoping that he couldn't see me, I would stir away, until it was just right! I used to wonder what difference it made to my dad how I ate it, as long as I enjoyed it!

My Mum would bake on Sundays, while she had the oven on for the Sunday dinner. She had a side oven next to the fire in the living room as well as a cooker in the kitchen. She made fruit and cheese scones, tea cakes, lovely fairy cakes with white icing and those different coloured sprinkles on top. The silver, ball bearing ones used to crack hard on my teeth, even so, I still used to eat them. None of her baked goodies lasted long. Those piping hot scones from the oven were to die for. We would be waiting for them to come out of the oven, ready to feast on them, slathering them in loads of butter. The smell through the house was lovely. Like a bakery. Sometimes, she would spend ages preparing a mountain of cheese and tomato and egg sandwiches, wrap them in greaseproof paper and put them in a silver tin. My Dad used to tell her to prepare a picnic and we would go off to the coast, or up to the moors for the day. It was always such a feast, and a treat, too, we had biscuits in wrappers on, like *Blue Ribbons* and *Kit Kats*, which we only got on special occasions, it felt like something from a *Famous Five* book...!

I had this favourite, pale yellow coloured dress, which had brown buttons and a pleated skirt. I wore a homemade yellow cardigan with it, especially for our day out. I loved that dress and I always felt posh in it. I used to call it my *custard dress* as it reminded me of a lovely bowl of the yellow sauce dessert. I had little frilly ankle socks, with black shiny shoes. Dina, Harry and I, would all get ready, then we'd sit to attention in the dining room as we waited to go on our trip out. Mum used to scrape Dina's hair back into a ponytail right on the top of her head. It looked really painful, Dina's eyebrows were always so high on her face that she looked like she'd had a face lift, or she was constantly in pain with a red forehead. My hair was always short and curly, I think my Mum used to cut it. Mum didn't usually wear much makeup, just a bit of powder on her face and red lipstick, especially when these trips were planned, and she'd splash on some of her favourite perfume.

Just before we were ready to go, nine times out of ten, Mum and Dad would have a humdinger of a row. After that, my dad would say we were not going to go on our trip. The row was usually over something silly like where would we park. Dad used to always worry about getting parked. He would often disappear off in the car to do a dummy run, to make sure he could safely park. I was devastated every time he would cancel the outing. *I hated being so let down and that flat feeling of disappointment it gave me.*

My Mum and Dad rowed a lot, usually over money, or cars. Dad kept buying dud cars that broke down and cost twice as much as they did when he bought them to repair. Eventually, after a huge shouting match, my Mum would storm out of the house, saying she was going to the hills. Dad had a terrible temper; I think it ran in his side of the family. After the explosion it was usual for Mum to disappear for a couple of hours, when she would return home and everything would be quiet, but it would be okay. She was good at sulking; she could keep it up for days. I always worried from the minute she left the house that she wouldn't come back, until I heard the door open, and she was back home again. Phew! Dina and I would sit at the top of the stairs listening to the rows. Occasionally, Dina would shout down to tell them to shut up and stop it. I never had the nerve to do that. She was much braver than me. After a while we got used to it. I came to the conclusion that it seemed normal that you had to go through a row before anything nice happened. Anyway, we would end up not going on our trip to the Dales, or the seaside, and we would go upstairs and get changed into our scruffy, homemade, clothes again. We would then eat the picnic in silence from the dining table at home. It never tasted as nice, though through an awkward atmosphere.

Sometimes on a Sunday afternoon, Harry would ask if we wanted him to do a disco. He would set up fairy lights in the dining room, along the top of the curtains, ready for the Top Twenty radio show to begin at 6pm. Dina and I would set up a buffet on the table, with *Marmite* and white bread, cut into fingers. We would stir up some custard mix and put it in egg cups as dessert... *yuck!* It was always much tastier when Mum heated it in a saucepan, but this was our cold, unsupervised, version! On the odd occasion, Mum and Dad would drive to a country pub, leaving us sitting in the car, in the pub car park. They would pop out to bring us a bag of crisps and bottle of pop each, to keep us quiet and entertained. That was a treat, I loved the crisps, we didn't get those often. They didn't stay long; it was about the only social thing they did together. Dad used to go out more than Mum, she would always stay at home with us, knitting weird, themed jumpers or dresses, she would watch *Come Dancing* on the Telly with Terry Wogan. Dad used to go out and meet up with his brothers. He had four of them, altogether. They went to the Working Men's Club. God knows how, but he must have driven there and back, as we lived miles away from anywhere. I'm pretty sure there would be no bus service in the evenings in those days and definitely no taxis. It seemed to me that Dad lived a very separate life sometimes. I don't think he was much of a family man in the early days, being more interested in cigarettes, cars and the Club. Maybe that's why they rowed.

Harry, my brother, was a very quiet and shy boy,about four years older than me. He would isolate himself a lot of the time, living with 2 sisters I think he preferred to be on his own. We didn't see much of him, so it was special for us when we did spend time with him on a Sunday night. Harry was very clever and would have made a really good journalist as he had a great interest in articles in the newspapers and magazines. He'd spend hours cutting out quotes and articles, etc.

Harry just about lived in his bedroom on his own and it seemed like my Mum and Dad just let him stay there on his own, not encouraging him to come downstairs, except for meals. They never encouraged him to mix with us, or do anything with us really, he was just left on his own, listening to the radio in his room and cutting out articles from music magazines. Looking back, he must have been happy with his own company, keeping away from the noise and chaos of 2 sisters.

A year or two later, Harry got a Saturday job in the butchers in the local town. I found out later from Mum that he did that to help her with finances. Dad wasn't giving her much housekeeping, she told me that Harry felt sorry for her and wanted to help. Mum seemed to be working all hours cleaning and, occasionally, slapping potato on plates as a dinner lady at the school, though we still didn't have enough money. Dad kept his own money, he just gave her weekly housekeeping, which clearly wasn't enough. One Saturday, while Harry was at work, the butcher told him to clean all the butcher's blocks in the back room. What a shit job. He was carrying a pail, full to the brim of scalding hot water, when he accidentally spilled it down his wellies. When it happened, we were out in the local town and the grocer took a call. Everyone knew each other and it was the butcher trying to find my Mum and Dad to tell them what had happened. The butcher told us that an ambulance had been called and Harry had been taken to the Burns Unit at a local Hospital. We rushed to the hospital, where they told us that Harry had lost almost all the top layers of the skin on his feet and lower legs. He was in hospital for weeks, having skin grafts, and I visited him once and he had his bottom half protected in what looked like a tent. He didn't say much about any of it. He was very brave and just go on with it. He didn't grumble or moan about it at all. He must have been in a lot of pain.

Harry didn't go back to work at the butchers and seemed to withdraw again spending most of his time on his own in his bedroom. He struggled with sweaty feet and from then on, he couldn't walk too far without his feet becoming very painful and swollen. Harry was and is a very witty person with a very dry sense of humour, yet it seemed like life was against him. I felt sorry for him. My clever big brother.

Chapter Two

Happy Days 1965

My Mum was a cleaner in the village, she had jobs at two places, the first was for a gay couple, Miss Ramsden and Miss Bentley. They seemed a bit weird to me, it wasn't public knowledge that they were gay, in those days, the term 'gay' was related to someone being happy. Nobody spoke about them in that way. It was the unmentionable. Anyway, they had two bungalows joined together with a door in the middle, which meant that they could come and go into each other's place. Miss Bentley used to dress in what looked like a man's suit, she had mega short hair and wore very male type glasses, she looked just like a bloke. I often wondered what she was. Miss Ramsden was fat, she used to wear similar heavy tartan clothes, but wore a skirt instead of trousers. I remember being a bit scared of them both. They were different. One day, I had beans on toast at their house, I don't know why, but that has stuck in my mind. Funny what you remember.

My Mum used to clean at the local pub as well and we used to go with her sometimes, at that time we thought it was really posh in their private flat above the bar because they had a bar in their lounge and big white leather settees, very Austin Powers. It was quite tacky really but at that time it was the in thing. We would often get a bag of chips from the pub kitchen for our lunch, so I wasn't complaining. Mum also used to look after three girls for her friend, our adopted Auntie Maggie. She was a teacher, who worked at a deaf school. She didn't seem very maternal at all. She was always very pleased to dump the kids on us and she would even do it sometimes at the weekends when she wasn't working, just so she could have a break! It was my Mum that needed the break not her! Harry used to hate it when the girls came, three days a week for the whole day in the holidays. He used to say "are those girls coming again" through gritted teeth. Poor lad surrounded by screaming girls. No wonder he withdrew to his bedroom. I used to play with Belinda, the youngest one, she had long, ginger hair and a million freckles on her face, Catrina was the oldest and we thought she was weird as she wore big thick glasses with dense lenses, and she had quite short hair and just wanted to read books. She became a doctor. Hermione was the middle one. I always thought she was a right little bitch, with long brown hair. She used to cause all sorts of trouble, ironically, she became a Police Inspector! My Mum used to be exhausted and breathed a sigh of relief when they had gone home. She worked so hard every day. I think she got about £3 a week for having them! Bonkers!

My Dad was a farmer at heart. He loved the countryside; he was very proud to be from the North. He was brought up by his mother's brother, his Uncle Gregory, on his farm. I am not sure why, but for some reason, his mother couldn't cope with all of her sons and so it was agreed that Dad would go to live with Uncle Gregory. Maybe Dad was the naughty one. He would help his uncle to run the family farm, The Mill, he would plough the fields with two large Clydesdale horses. When his uncle died, a local man offered to buy the Mill and asked Dad to be the farm manager, which meant that he could carry on running the farm that he loved. Dad declined the offer, as he didn't have the confidence to take it on. My Mum was keen for him to do it, but he refused. Once my dad made his mind up, it was never spoken about again.

Dad became a milkman for a local dairy firm. He used to get up really early six days a week to deliver the milk. By coincidence, he was called Ernie, and when *Benny Hill* released that song, *Ernie the fastest milkman in the West*, which became my dad's song! He had one of those old fashioned, electronic milk floats, with a tiny cab and open sides. I thought he was different as he used to sell those little bottles of orange juice as well and, sometimes, he'd sell yoghurts and eggs. He worked really hard, smoked like a chimney at that time and I didn't see much of him really. I was always a bit scared of him.

Probably because in times of stress my Mum used to say, wait until your dad gets home, I'll tell him what you have been up to, which was usually nothing. I used to dread him coming home. Sometimes, Dad would take the three of us with him to get the eggs to sell on the van, we went across the moors to the farm, there were loads of hens all stuck in these great big huts with lights on, now I know they were *battery hens*, though back then it did seem very cruel to me and still does today. They were all crammed in, with feathers and beaks sticking out of the cages. The place stank of sweaty socks, too! When Dad came home, he used to have his tea at the same time every day and then fall asleep in his armchair and snore very loudly all evening. Dad was always very tired.

Mum would knit jumpers for us all, sitting in the living room, and we would sit on the floor. We didn't have enough chairs for everyone to sit down. If we had visitors, we would use the emergency chairs from Mum's bedroom. Sometimes on a Saturday night Harry would come downstairs and spend time with us in the lounge. Mum and Dad would have done the Friday night big shop so we would all hope for treats. We loved it, sharing a big bag of pick and mix sweets, frutella's which were a firm favourite. Harry being the oldest kid was always in charge of sharing them out into five bags, one bag each, I'm sure he always made sure he got all the strawberry frutella's and I would get the crap mango or pineapple ones! I didn't care and used to make mine last the whole week until next time. I couldn't do that now; they'd be gone in five minutes. How times change! Mum gave us Ski Yoghurts, too, they were shaped like little milk churns. I used to ask for one of those and make it last two days! Special things like them always went very quickly in our house, I used to make them last as long as possible. Dina used to find that very annoying, it seemed like she would gobble up her treats within minutes, then she'd try and eat mine. I suppose that's a bit like me now, buying things for best and never wearing them. Weird.

Despite the rows, those were happy days, spent mostly amusing myself with my dolls, or at the farm with Lizzie, making houses out of pigsties. I was a girly girl, I loved to dress up and home build with Lizzie. I didn't spend much time with Dina, even though we shared a bedroom. We were quite different. I always remember her side of the bedroom being like a tip, while mine was spotlessly tidy and organised. It used to irritate me when she just dropped her clothes on the floor, and when she'd finished her homework or reading, how she'd just snuggle down in her bed that would be covered with books and clothes! Sometimes, I wasn't even sure if she was in there, until there was a thud on the floor when one of her books had slipped of the bed when she turned over. We were like chalk and cheese when we were young. I used to love putting on those shows with Lizzie and making people laugh, we organised them regularly. It was a chance for Mum to take a break from the chores and come over to watch. Mum and Auntie Alicia would drink gallons of tea, chuckling away at us. We would be dressed up to the nines, in our big, floaty dresses and hats, and wearing red lipstick, thinking we were so very special. Such happy days.

Most Saturdays we went to our grandma's house, she was Mum's mother, then we'd move on to one of Mum's sister's houses. She had three sisters. May, Ava and Jennie. Auntie May had two adopted kids, Seren and Tyrone, Tyrone was a cheeky little kid, always in trouble. Seren was very quiet. Aunt Ava had a daughter Julie, she was quiet and didn't have much to do with us, she was the same age as Dina, and I think there was some rivalry there. Auntie Jennie had one daughter, Jeanette, a big girl who blushed a lot, she always seemed like she was such a bag of nerves. They all lived in the next village away from us, though they were quite near to each other, that's why we would always start off at that grandma's house. As Grandma lived near a fish and chip shop, we'd usually have fish and chips at her house out of the newspaper, sometimes followed with one of those tinned treacle puddings and custard. Goodness knows how they used to make one of those go around all of us, but they did. I could gobble a whole one to myself now. I loved that pudding. It was lovely, well it must have been, because I never forgot it! We would stay at Grandma's for most of the day. After dinner, us kids would go outside and play in the churchyard, it was just next to her house. Sometimes, we went home via my Auntie Jennie's house for tea. Auntie Jennie and her husband, Uncle Alvin, lived in a small cottage, which was tied to his job. He was a gamekeeper and he always had guns in the house and dead game in the back garden. The cottage was a tip. Uncle Alvin used to zoom around on a black motorbike in black leather clothing, I was very nervous around him. He once showed me a bucket full of water outside the back door, it was full of dead kittens. He had drowned them; I was so upset. He just laughed. There was a sinister side to him.

Auntie Jennie used to belittle Jeanette, by taking the piss out of her being big. She used to grumble about how fat Jeanette was, yet still allow her to eat huge, pork pies when they went to the butcher's shop. She'd eat it outside, then eat a whole packet of Jaffa cakes by herself in the back of the car on the way home. Auntie

Jennie must have been a feeder. It didn't make any sense to me; I was very thin. I once overheard Auntie Jennie and my Mum saying that I was too thin, there must be something wrong with me. I used to eat, but not much. I was worried after that, in case there was actually something wrong with me.

Very occasionally, on a Sunday, we would go to my other Grandma, she was my Dad's Mum. She used to make lovely, soggy, Yorkshire puddings, with lots of onion gravy, and bake tea cakes that we would bring home with us to eat for our tea, later on. If we went there on a Saturday, the grownups used to watch the Saturday afternoon racing and some of my dad's brothers would have a bet at the local bookies. The men smelled of beer. It was always exciting, watching the race, in case one of them had a winner. Most of the time, they didn't, of course. We would play in the garden, or on the floor behind their chairs. I would spend time sitting on my Uncle Bernie's knee, he was my godfather. He died of a heart attack in his early forties, I don't remember much about him, apart from the fact that he had great, big brown eyes, he looked tanned, and he seemed troubled. I missed him when he was gone. I found him strange, though I liked him.

Chapter Three

A Horse called Thomas Wood 1970

Our lovely little world changed when my dad got a new job in Hackness. The position came with, what was then known as, a tied house. I remember the day we moved in, the house was filthy, my Mum spent all day cleaning everything. She was so house proud; she'd clean until you could see your face in the wooden floors after she'd finished. We needed to move on, as my dad was well known in the village, and it turned out that there was gossip going around that he had a fling with a local girl, who was much younger than him. She worked in a newsagent shop. One day, after Dad's blip came out, Mum took me to the shop where the girl worked. Awkward. I sensed something was wrong but didn't know what it was at the time. It was years later when my Mum and I talked about it. There was such a weird atmosphere in the house, I did not understand it at the time, of course, now I do. The tension at home was terrible. Nobody could settle. My parents decided that it would be best for Dad to look for work out of the area. I didn't know this at the time, and I've never actually been told the official reason for the change. 'officially' been told. My sister, Dina, was told though and she passed it on to me later on. I think Dina had found out somehow and they were forced to tell her what had happened.

Mum and Dad's relationship was always strained, now it was even worse. I'd often wonder why, and as I said, they never told me. My parents constantly picked and poked at each other, I always felt my Mum was holding a grudge against my dad, which she clearly was. He seemed to irritate her all the time, she would snap at him, he'd lose his temper then, very quickly. It was like they were both on high alert and ready to row in an instant. Must have been guilt or something. Instead of splitting up, they decided to move out of the village to Hackness and start afresh. The problem was that Mum could not forgive Dad. Looking back now, I feel that she should have left him, though that was just not an option in those days. Mum stayed and they were both miserable. Mum and Dad were fond of Hackness as it was where they'd spent their honeymoon, ironic really. Before they were married, they used to go to Hackness for holidays, to stay with my Dad's Auntie Dot and Uncle Gerry. They spent many good times in Hackness, it seemed to be the obvious choice for Dad's escape from his alleged mistake.

I remember Auntie Dot had a lovely dog called

Major, a golden Labrador. We would disappear out through the cellar door to play with him on the green, which is area of protected grass spread around in different parts of Hackness. Our Aunt and Uncle lived in a three storey, terraced house, I remember it being dark and quite cramped, with very old-fashioned décor. The cellar was our favourite place to hide and play.

So, Dad had an interview for a job as a Farm Manger at the Hackness Equestrian Centre. He missed his farming life, which was his passion really. He should never have become a bloody milkman. He drove us all with him to Hackness for the interview and while Dad was doing his best to impress the Major who owned the Centre, we spent all the time, over two hours, sitting in the car, outside in the car park, looking at the fields in front of us. The Major was a typical major, with his limp, he was wearing an old-fashioned pair of grey jodhpurs and a cap, with a tweed waistcoat and jacket. He always wore a tie, just like my dad did. The Major smoked a pipe that always seemed to be unlit and hanging out of his mouth, even when he was out riding. At the interview, my dad never introduced my Mum to the Major. Afterwards, she was fuming again, as she sat in the car, with a stern look on her face, she looked like she was going to burst. I found that a bit weird of Dad, considering he was moving us all to a new place. I wondered if he was ashamed of us, we were a motley crew, with our homemade clothes on. Bit like the Beverley Hill Billies off the telly show.

Dad always seemed to need to impress people. The Centre was a nice place, the business was mainly horses and they offered riding lessons and, of course, they had the liveries, which brought in the main focus and income. The Major offered Dad the Farm Manager role and he accepted it. After a while, it became clear that he was, in fact, just a glorified stable hand/handyman, which was way below his qualifications, as an established and competent farmer. We started to call the Major the boss, which is how everyone there referred to him, we simply joined in. Dad spent most of his time maintaining the fields, fences, stables and grounds. One of his main duties there was the muck heap, he used to get up really early to go and help with the mucking out of the horses. He would ride around the stable yard on a tractor, with a bucket on it, for scooping all the shit into the big trailer, ready for it to be taken away. He was proud of his muck and was almost territorial over it and the way it was stacked. Sad really, Dad was such a perfectionist, even the shit had to be placed in the correct way! He stunk of it.

When Dad first started his job there was a small herd of bullocks. Sometimes on a Sunday afternoon, I went with him on the tractor and trailer, across what seemed like loads of fields, to feed them with hay. He would keep driving as I chucked the hay over the side for them. They didn't last long before they were sent off for slaughter, then Dad's job was diminished even further, as he had much less responsibility than he deserved, having had all his farming experience. I am sure that he regretted the move, though he was a proud and stubborn man, he'd never admit it, instead he always said he was totally happy. Dad seemed to be making the best out of a bad situation. On the other hand, Mum wasn't so happy. I don't think she ever forgave my dad for dragging us all away from our family and friends which clearly wasn't a totally joint decision. She was quite serious when he was at home, always with a stern expression on her face. She deliberately didn't laugh at the same things as him on TV, if he said it was black, she would say it was white. Dad liked Shirley Bassey, my Mum, of course, hated her. She must have been jealous of old Shirley! Mum was determined never to show any interest whatsoever in Dad's work, or the people involved in it. It was wrong. It would have been better for Mum if she had stayed at the village with us and left him, if she felt so strongly against him. Their relationship was always stormy, though now it was even worse, at a time when we were all feeling like fish out of water, and we were homesick for the village and our family and friends there. Our parents should have been pulling us all together, instead it seemed we were all going our separate ways.

One day, Dad suggested I went with him up to 'the Centre', as it became known. I wasn't particularly interested in horses; I was actually quite scared of them. They were huge things. I didn't know anyone really round there, I was feeling miserable at school, too. I was lonely and bored, and I decided to go along with Dad for something to do. Also, I'd always been scared of my dad, so when he suggested I do something with him, I didn't want to refuse. When we got there, he went off to mend some fences or something, I was left wandering around on my own. I was in the pony stables looking at them, when I got talking to a girl called Sandie. She seemed to know completely what she was doing and was chatting away with me, while she was tacking up one of the ponies, ready for a riding lesson. She suggested I helped her. It was after that when we became very good friends. Sandie was my age; she spent her summer holidays and weekends helping out at the Centre. We started to work our little arses off to get a ride, in return for all our hard work. They definitely got a good deal, as it was very cheap labour for them, as they didn't actually pay us. After a while every spare minute we had, we spent at the Centre with the ponies, we would go after school. Sandie lived about a mile away in a village nearby, she would ride her bike up and I would run beside her, I didn't have a bike. Sometimes she would give me a croggy. It was such fun.

We would go at the crack of dawn in the morning to catch the ponies, who lived out in the fields, then we'd muck out the ones that lived in. Funny how I struggled to get up for school during the week but as soon as the weekend came, I was up like a lark! When we arrived at the Centre, we checked the list of the ponies needed for the day on the main notice board. We had to make sure that all the ponies that were being used that day were groomed, clean and tacked up, in time for their lessons. We ran it like clockwork. We absolutely loved it, I felt really important and like I was needed. In return we got our free rides and after a while we both became very confident riders. We used to ride in local cross country and show jumping events and those held at the Centre. We would also help out at the shows, we were on duty at the show jumping arena, putting the jumps back up when the horses had knocked them down. Eventually I managed to get a weekend job in the kitchen, too. I would squeeze that in during the morning and then go back outside in the afternoon. I got £3 for the weekend. I used to have to do some of the cleaning around the place as well, though I didn't care, I just loved being there. It made me feel important,

I liked that. I used to throw together great big bowls of homemade soup. I had a knack for it. I watched my Mum make soup out of old bones and lentils, I copied her.

Harry hated the move more than any of us, he never went to the Centre, or showed any interest in it, at all. He still claims, with victory, that he never set foot on Centre land. That became Harry's slogan, he was very proud of it. Actually, it was the worst time in Harry's life for us to move, he had just got back on his feet from his accident and was doing well at the Grammar School, then had to leave right in the middle of his GCSE's. He took it very badly. He really didn't want to move. Dad and Harry hardly spoke. Harry couldn't settle in Hackness and eventually started at college to study. He is extremely quick witted, with a very dry sense of humour. He would have made a really good journalist.

Dina and I went to a local High School, I hated it. I was extremely shy, I blushed for no reason, and got the piss taken out of me by older, more confident, girls with boobs and makeup, which made me feel even worse. I was chased around the corridors by a bunch of awful boys when they found out my middle name. They were chanting abuse at me. I was mortified, I hid in the toilets until they had gone. It really upset me and it's not surprising that I really didn't like secondary school and would have done anything I could to get out of going there. Dina, on the other hand, made friends quite easily and settled in.

She was much more confident than me, she made friends very quickly. Later on, though, she got in with the wrong crowd when she was in the fourth year. She was starting to spend time with some older biker friends outside school. It felt like she used to disappear for days on end, often going camping in fields. Dina was a feisty teenager. My Dad would spend ages driving around late at night, trying to find her. I always felt as though she was Dad's favourite kid. He had pet names for her when she was younger. Dina rebelled for a few months around that time, it was very tough at home to be honest. We were very different kids. It was of course a phase she was going through like so many kids her age at that time. I envied her spirit in some ways and wished I had her confidence and popularity. I was so God damn shy.

When one of our cousins was getting married, we all insisted that Dina attend the wedding with us, and she did. Remarkably, something must have clicked with her on that day, as she suddenly seemed to change it was almost like she had been away! Next thing we knew, she had managed to become head girl for the whole of her fifth and final year at school. I think that shows just how clever my sister could be, when she wanted to be. I was so proud of her.

Over time I became friends with Sarah, who was one of the riding instructors at the Centre. She had a beautiful, grey gelding, called Thomas Wood, and I started to look after him for her. Sarah was always really busy, either teaching, or riding one of the Centre's horses, and she didn't seem to have much time for Thomas. Ridiculous as it may seem, I fell in love with this lovely horse! I used to spend all my spare time with Thomas and Sarah saw the connection between us. After a while, Sarah suggested that I should exercise him for her, to help him get fit for the upcoming events and show jumping competitions. I started to look after him most of the time for her. Weekends and after school, I used to love taking him out for hacks and down to the field, working him round the dressage ring. It felt as if Thomas belonged to me, and I couldn't wait to see him. Thomas would be waiting for me every weekend, when he saw me come around the corner he would weave from side to side, throwing his head around in delight, he would whinny gently and mumble through his nostrils. He was so gorgeous. At the end of the weekend, I used to lie down with him in the stable, he was just like a big teddy bear. I really did love him. I trusted him, completely. Sarah eventually sold Thomas and it broke my heart. I wanted desperately to buy him; we just didn't have the cash. Thomas was an event horse, Sarah wanted a smaller, more stocky type of horse, and she wasn't that close to him. She didn't have the same connection we had, I thought she was almost ruthless about selling him and cold hearted. Maybe that was the way she coped with it. I don't know.

I will never forget the day Thomas left. They lead him into the horsebox. As they drove him away, he managed to turn his head and I swear he looked right at me, he was neighing, almost as if he was saying goodbye to me. I was in tears. Sarah never even blinked. She just turned and walked away. I never saw him again. I was completely lost, I felt I couldn't go to the stables anymore. I missed him so much. I used to walk up and down the lane where we lived and just cry my eyes out. It was the first time I had felt such a loss, I never thought I would feel like that again. How wrong could I have been.

Chapter Four

Donovan 'Bloody' Gregg 1977

Dad decided he'd had enough of his job. He wasn't happy being a glorified farm hand, things had become sour between him and the Major. Dad got pissed off, he secured another job at the local council, as a groundsman for the schools in the area, his duties included some general maintenance work. We would, of course, have to move out of the tied house and go into a council house in Hackness. Sadly, my riding days came to an end, as it was way too far for me to go to the stables. Anyway, everyone I had known there had moved on to different things, too. I suppose that was my childhood fun, now it was time to grow up, get a job and venture out into the real world. Leaving school, just before my seventeenth birthday, I had no clue what I wanted to do. Most of my friends had signed up for a two-year secretarial course at the Local College of Further Education. I joined them, despite having no interest in becoming a secretary. I knew that I definitely didn't want to work in a shop, or become a hairdresser, or whatever else was on offer back then. The secretarial course seemed like the most sensible thing to do, especially with my lack of qualifications. I wasn't the Brain of Britain, I used to fall apart in exams, no matter how much revision I did, nothing seemed to go in!

I was incapable of concentrating long enough to be able to read a book, I would stare at the words, but I'd be thinking of lots of other things. After a while, I'd give up and put the book down. Same with exams, as soon as I opened the paper and looked at the questions, I went completely blank. Couldn't remember anything at all until about five minutes before the end of the exam time, when some things would come back to me. Too late. Deep down I knew I wasn't ready to start work yet, and College seemed like the best thing to do at the time. Ideally, I would have liked to have stayed in the world of horses, but becoming a groom was about my only option, though I didn't have the courage to do that as it would have meant leaving home, which I certainly wasn't ready to do. My confidence was very low. I had looked into careers with horses, I had even got an interview to work with an International Showjumper. Dad encouraged me; he took me for the interview. I hadn't a clue what I was doing, I turned up in jeans and heeled ankle boots. Of course, they wanted to see my riding skills, for which I was completely unprepared. They put me on one of their fantastic showjumpers. I actually managed to control the horse and took it over some very high jumps. I was shitting myself, but I did it, heels and all. I didn't get the job though, which did zero for my confidence levels. I binned the whole idea. My Dad seemed disappointed, though I think he knew I wasn't ready to leave home anyway. My heart was still broken from losing Thomas. I was still sad about that, and I had no idea what path to take, the secretarial course seemed like a good option at the time.

I was still quite shy and quiet in a crowd, though I came out of my shell a bit when I started the course. I made a few friends, we started to all go out together at weekends, socialising in Hackness. I was very shy, especially around boys, I only used to drink half a lager and I'd be pissed. I remember my first kiss. We were at a Nightclub probably on a student night. It was the end of the night, and I was slow dancing and smooching with this boy one minute, the next I thought I was going to choke when he put his tongue down my throat! I didn't much like that, and he was a very sloppy kisser. I felt my first romantic encounter wasn't all it was cracked up to be, as I emerged from the dance floor, feeling like I was covered in slobber and my face was soaked with it! I thought I was in love; this guy would be my husband! I never saw him again!

I kept in touch with Sandie from the stables, we used to meet up to go to Student night at the Nightclub most Wednesday nights. Sandie was more of a student type than me. She was very popular with the boys, she was really slim, looked great in jeans and a casual shirt, with a leather belt. She had a sort of German look about her, very olive skin and dark brown eyes, with sandy blonde short hair. She didn't need to wear makeup, though sometimes she'd put on a bit of blusher and blue eyeliner. In the summer holidays, her parents used to go away for a couple of weeks, of course, Sandie and her brothers didn't want to go with them, and I'd move in to stay with them. We had a ball; we were off the leash. Party time. One night, when we managed to get an invite to a house party at the other side of town, Sandie decided to bring a bottle of vodka with us. The bottle did not make it to the party and neither did we. Sandie drank most of it on the way there and not being much of a drinker usually, she seemed to turn into a different person. She became nasty, shouting at me, saying I was no friend of hers. She was falling into hedges and stumbling all over the place, it was a nightmare. Though I realised it was probably the drink talking, I was hurt by the way she'd reacted. I didn't really understand the evils of drink at that age, I just took it to heart. No matter how I tried I couldn't seem to get through to her. She just kept lashing out at me. Eventually, I decided to leave her with some other friends, I walked back to her house on my own. I could not sleep; I was too riddled with guilt. It was very late when I heard Sandie stumble through the back door. I went downstairs to see her, she was spark out, fast asleep, face down on the kitchen floor. I couldn't wake her up, I decided it was best to leave her there, I got a pillow and her quilt off her bed, leaving her to sleep it off. Next morning, Sandie couldn't remember any of it, she was in a hell of a state. She was throwing up and could hardly speak. She had really poisoned herself, she had absolutely no memory of the night after we'd set off for the party. Goodness knows how she got herself home, she couldn't remember! I thought it served her right, for being so vicious to me.

Despite that episode we remained good friends. After College finished, Sandie decided to go to Agricultural College at Baverstock and eventually we drifted apart over time. In an attempt to keep in touch, she invited me to stay for the weekend, I think there was some sort of young farmers event on at the College. I agreed to go, though as soon as I got there, I regretted it. Inevitably, Sandie had made loads of new friends, I just felt like I didn't fit in, and she was different now. It was clear we didn't have the same interests anymore. We did keep in touch after that and when she came home in the summer holidays, we were sitting at her dining room table, listening to the radio, when the news came on saying that Elvis had died. I think that was the last summer I spent with Sandie. Later, when she got a job as a farm secretary in Barford St Martin, she moved permanently. She is still there now, married, and she has two boys. We keep in touch on birthdays, at Christmas, and that's about it. We are very different people, though she will always be in my heart.

Amazingly, I somehow managed to scrape my way through the two years' secretarial course at college. I didn't really like it, though it was better than getting a full-time job that I was sure I would not like. When we did shorthand class, I found that I was super quick at squiggling it all down, I could catch each phrase. Only one problem, I could never read it back – oops! I really enjoyed the audio typing class, where we practiced on those really old-fashioned Olivetti typewriters, the ones with a block of wood placed over the keyboard, which stopped you from seeing the keys. This technique helped to make me a really fast touch typist. There was such a racket in that room, as we all bashed away on the heavy keyboards. I remember using carbon copies and Tippex. What a ball ache!
I met a couple of girls at college, though we didn't really keep in touch after we left. Debbie was one of them, she was really pretty, looked like a doll, short curly blonde hair with bright blue eyes, super white teeth and rosy cheeks. I was always a bit nervous around her as she

was a diabetic. When we first met, the first thing she did was give me strict instructions about the procedures I would need to undertake, if she collapsed with a diabetic fit. I was horrified! Consequently, most of the time I spent with her, I was on edge, wondering if I could remember what to do. Sort of spoilt the friendship, really! When I left College, I still didn't know which direction I wanted to take, as I didn't really have the confidence to take a secretarial job, and I didn't really want to. I had got good qualifications, thinking it would be something I would rather do when I was a lot older. I was getting pressure from home to find something. Eventually I saw an advert in the local paper for a dental nurse/receptionist, it was a training position. This interested me, I applied for the job, and, to my surprise, I got it. As it turned out, the Dentist had horses, and in my riding days I had seen his daughter competing at local events, I had heard of the family already. I think that swung it for the Dentist, as he loved to brag about his daughter and their horses. I quite enjoyed the job, though I didn't like anaesthetic day, every Friday morning, for extractions. One time, I nearly fainted, after that, I was excused from my dental nurse duties, instead, I worked on reception on extraction days. The older nurse used to take care of the patients who had a general anaesthetic. She really enjoyed it. She was a bit of a military type, nothing scared her! I didn't like seeing people under those circumstances, especially the children, as it reminded me of the time, I had to have six teeth out. I had struggled and fought with the Dentist, grabbing his wrist, until I went under. It was awful, I felt like I was being killed, I never forgot it, or the taste of the rubber when they put that cube in patient's mouths, to stop them clenching their teeth shut. Watching the small children in that situation was not good for me as it was a trigger for flashback memories. I don't think it was particularly encouraging for them either, seeing the nurse looking horrified, doesn't instil much confidence, does it?!

One day, a lovely girl called Hazel started working with us, she was the junior nurse. Hazel and I instantly hit it off, we got along really well. We began to spend most of our lunchtimes together, in the nurses' rest room. Hazel was very funny, she really made me laugh. One lunchtime, we were sitting and chatting, as we looked out of the window, when all of a sudden, she jumped up.

Hazel blurted out, "Oh my God, it's Donovan bloody Gregg and I'm not kidding!"

She pointed out of the window. I looked out to see who she was talking about. The man in question was walking across the gardens, opposite the surgery, towards our building. I asked her who he was and said he looked nice. Hazel told me Donovan was a bit weird, nobody knew much about him, he was a proper dark horse. Naturally, I was instantly intrigued, wanting to know more. He had an appointment at 2pm. I brushed my hair, put on more lippy and went out to reception. When Donovan came in, I opened up the sliding window on the reception counter and he told me he had an appointment now. I tried not to, yet I couldn't help blushing as I told him to take a seat, we won't be long. I hid my face with my hair, something I did often, when I was embarrassed. Composing myself, as the Dentist buzzed through and asked me to bring the next patient to him. I sat at the desk beside Donovan, making the relevant notes, while the dentist checked his teeth and gums. He didn't need any treatment, the Dentist just gave him a scale and polish, as I used a machine to suck all the slobber out of his mouth and I had to sit closer next to him. Every time our eyes met, I would look away, he did the same. It was a very weird feeling; I suppose that was the chemistry that was charging between us. The Dentist sensed it and pulled my leg when Donovan had left the surgery, much to my embarrassment.

I felt an overwhelming urge to see him before he left, I followed him out of the surgery. I was panicking when he was leaving, because I might not see him again, as he didn't need to any treatment for another six months. I wanted to see him one more time. I pretended I needed to get something from the surgery at the top of the stairs. I got to the door, and he was at the bottom of the stairs. He turned to look up at me, giving me a lovely smile as he said goodbye. I smiled back at him and said bye back. My heart actually missed a beat. I was hooked. I felt I had no choice but to try and see him again.

It turned out that Hazel's boyfriend, Dev, was one of Donovan's group of friends and Hazel told Dev all about our encounter, they decided to set Donovan and I up on a kind of date or night out. A couple of weeks later, on a Friday night, I went out with Hazel, and we went to a few pubs. We were looking for Dev and his friends, I was excited as I knew that Donovan was going to be there, too. By mid-evening, though, there was no sign of the lads, I was beginning to give up hope. We walked past the town car park and spotted the car they were using. I scribbled a note reading, *'there's no limit to where we will be in the city tonight'* and Hazel put it under the windscreen wiper. When we arrived at the club, it was pretty dead. We bought drinks and sat down, still hopeful that they would show up. In those days there weren't any mobile phones, there was no chance of texting or calling, we just had to live in hope! Anyway, after a while, they all walked in, Donovan included. He looked really nice, he was tall and dark, he had lovely, big, brown eyes, that always looked slightly watery. He was playing it cool; it took a while for him to talk to me. He wore a brown suit, with a white shirt, and a brown tie. I was really nervous, I liked him very much. I thought he would not look twice at me. I lacked confidence, it was really difficult for me to open up and talk to him. I thought I wasn't good enough for him. When Donovan did, finally, come over to me, I couldn't believe it. We started talking. At the end of the night, I gave him my home phone number. I didn't expect him to call me, though I was really hoping he would. Every time the phone rang, I prayed it was him. It wasn't.

A couple of weeks passed. As I expected, he didn't call me. I must have given him the wrong number, I thought. As Valentine's Day was looming, I decided to bite the bullet and send him a false tooth through the post. I wrapped it up in cotton wool and packed it into a box to send to him. I got his address from his dental records in the office. What I didn't realise was that Donovan had a similar idea. He was an optical technician at that time and while I was wrapping up a false tooth for him, he was wrapping up a lens for me! He put it into a box with a note, saying, *Meet me under the clock at the bus station at 8pm on Valentine's Day*. I was over the moon when I received that little box. I couldn't believe it, he actually liked me. How romantic. I was about to meet my first proper boyfriend. Woohoo!

Valentine's Day fell on a Saturday that year, it was ideal as it meant I had all day to get ready for our date! I was really nervous, I had to stop myself for getting there two hours' earlier at 6pm! I didn't want to be too keen. We met, as arranged, under the clock. It was lovely. After our first date, we started to see each other regularly. Once or twice a week, he would come round to my house and listen to music. Sometimes, we met up at the babbling brook down the road from me, Donovan was quite romantic. We would always meet up on Saturday nights, when we would go out and see a group of his friends at his local pub. I was in total awe of him, I couldn't believe he liked me.

Donovan lived in digs, when we met. He told me that he didn't want me to go there, as it was a dingy place, more like a bedsit, and he hated his landlord. In time, he really opened up to me, sharing that he had been adopted when he was a baby. He explained that although he seemed to have had a decent upbringing and didn't want for much, he had never really felt that he belonged to anyone or had anything of his own. He would fill up when he told me those sorts of things. I felt sorry for him. Donovan was always struggling for money, he never seemed happy, he seemed old before his time. He used to say he was looking forward to getting old. He was living in one room in a terraced house in Hackness, with his breakfast and evening meal provided for in his rent. He would complain all the time about the food there, it was always soaked in oil and fat, he said it was almost inedible. When I often suggested we went out of a meal for a change, Donovan said he'd already paid for his food in with the rent, and he preferred not to out for meals. He was quite tight, reluctant to spend his money. I was a working girl, I paid for myself, sometimes I paid for him, when I could.

We used to go to the cinema on a Sunday night. It was a cheap night out and we enjoyed it. One time, we went to see *The Exorcist* with some friends, they all took crucifixes with them to ward off the spirits. Everyone was frightened to death. I thought it was a right load of old tosh. It didn't bother me at all. Strange, as I used to be nervous of my own shadow. Maybe I had realised it was not real, just smoke and mirrors. Donovan was one of those that took a crucifix with him. I think he thought I was thick, as I wasn't scared. My Mum usually baked on a Sunday in those days, and I would pinch a load of cakes and scones, putting them into a Tupperware box for Donovan. I loved to give him that box of goodies, I hoped that he didn't just chuck them away on the way home. The cakes would last him for the week, until Mum baked again. I wanted desperately to help him and make him happy. He seemed to have had such a tough time, I just wanted to make things right for him and give him some sort of security and love.

Donovan had been adopted by the Gregg family. Nigel Gregg was a teacher and Pip Gregg was a secretary at the local police station. I would say they were middle class and not particularly short of money. He had a brother, Craig, and a sister, Violet. He told me that Craig always used to rub it in that Donovan had been adopted, and he used to respond with, "Well they chose me, they didn't choose you." They never really got along, Craig was gay, and Donovan didn't like that. He did get on well with Violet though. Sadly, when Donovan was sixteen, his adopted Mum, Pip, committed suicide. According to Donovan she used to drink heavily, he always felt guilty in some way, as she would send him to get her sherry from the off license. He told me that Pip was having an affair with one of the policemen at work. This man promised her that he would leave his wife and they would be together. Of course, it was just a line and rubbish, when Pip found out, she couldn't cope. Nigel was also having an affair, he had left Pip to move in with his lover, Elana. Donovan hated her, blaming her for their split and Pip's unhappiness. Nigel's betrayal was the final straw for Pip. She was found dead on a park bench in the Valley Gardens, right opposite to the house where Nigel and Elana were living. Pip had taken tablets, swilled down with booze.

Pip had pushed a note through Nigel's door, before she took the pills. Donovan never knew what she had written in the note, though he heard that it was not clear whether she actually intended to go through with it, and maybe it was more like a cry for help. Donovan thought it was a cry for help.

He didn't want to admit to himself that she would leave him. It hit him very hard, he used to say that was the second woman to let him down, his birth mother gave him up and then his adopted one killed herself. His opinion of women, particularly mothers, was low. When he told me all this, I just wanted to make everything right for him and felt desperately sorry for him yet again. Violet didn't really get on with Nigel or Pip, she had left home when she was about fifteen. She didn't seem to give a toss about her mother dying, according to Donovan. Craig was devastated, as he struggled with it immensely. It didn't bring the three of them closer, if anything, it made them more distant from each other, and all the siblings were definitely distant towards Nigel and Elana.

We used to go to the local pub every Saturday night, as all Donovan's friends would be there. I used to be very quiet. Donovan became very loud and opinionated when he drank a couple of drinks, he would delight in kicking off a debate between the women and the men. He would then sit back and watch everyone falling out and the carnage he'd caused. It was like he had struck a match and thrown it on a bonfire. He would sit there with a victorious look on his face, roll up fag in one hand and his other arm outstretched, as it rested on his knee, as if his mission to cause trouble between the couples was now completed. He often made me feel really small if I joined in the conversation. I felt like my opinions were always stupid when I saw his reaction to them. He would just glare at me with a look of disgust. Eventually, I kept quiet to avoid the awkwardness. Apparently, people had thought, incorrectly, that I was a snob and I thought I was better than everyone else, as I never spoke or joined in. How wrong they were! I just didn't dare speak up; in case I said the wrong thing. I felt supressed and unable to be myself most of the time, however, I was still falling in love with Donovan. I thought that his behaviour was normal. Consequently, I didn't really make many friends at that time, my confidence was extremely low. I comforted myself with the thought that I had Donovan and that's all that was important to me.

Above all, I wanted to make him happy. I didn't want to disappoint him by saying the wrong thing, or appearing stupid, it was much easier to keep quiet. I was seventeen when I passed my driving test on the second attempt.

Donovan encouraged me to buy a car. His friend Loz worked at a garage, he told us that he could sort it out. I got swept away with it. I had saved up £500 for an old banger. Before I knew it, I had bought an old, white mini, and I loved this little car, even though I was definitely being used as I was now the designated driver. I did have fun with it though, we went to a fancy-dress party one night and I was driving the car dressed up as Kermit the Frog. The costume had a removable head, I put it on to save room in the car. I could hardly see through the eyes, yet I managed to get us there and back. God knows how we weren't stopped by the police. Donovan had refused to dress up, making me look even more ridiculous. Typical. I must have looked a right idiot. I was boiling hot all night in the furry suit, carrying my head around with me.

A few weeks later, I nearly killed myself in that car. I was going to pick up Donovan and came whizzing down the hill towards a roundabout when the brakes failed completely. Nothing happened at all. They were floppy. I just kept on pumping them and hoped and prayed that nothing was coming round the roundabout. Thank God there wasn't. I managed to swerve into the car park of a garage, just after the roundabout, as I pulled the handbrake on. I was terrified. After this incident, I decided to get rid of that car. Loz had ripped me off completely! Donovan, however, would not hear of it, he told me it must have been my fault. He told me that I was a crap driver anyway. I knew I wasn't, though I let it go. I didn't want to fall out with Donovan about it. It was going to cost more than the car was worth to fix it, I scrapped it instead and put it all down to a bad experience.

After a while of meeting up here there and everywhere we (or rather Donovan) decided it would be a good idea to get a flat together. Mum and Dad weren't too keen for me to move in with Donovan. Dad didn't like him much; they never really spoke to each other. My parents didn't really try to stop me, even if they had, I wouldn't have listened to them. Donovan and I moved into a one bedroomed flat in Hackness. We could easily afford it, as I was still working at the dentist, he was still an optical technician. I didn't like Donovan being in the digs as he was very unhappy. I felt guilty that I was still living at home, being looked after by my Mum, us moving in together was a no brainer to me as I hoped that Donovan would finally be happy.

We'd been living there for a while when Donovan started to talk about the possibility of finding his real mother. I had my doubts about it but just wanted him to be settled and happy. At the time, thinking it would help him if he did track her down. I encouraged him and did all I could to help. When Donovan was eighteen, Nigel had given him all his adoption papers. Almost like he was washing his hands of Donovan. Ever since, Donovan could not settle as he felt compelled to find his birth mother.

He wanted to try and make sense of why she had given him away, in fact, he was desperate to know what had happened, to make her do that. We contacted Social Services, telling them that we wanted to trace Donovan's mother. They told us that the process should be taken very slowly and not to rush into doing anything. They allocated Donovan a Social Worker to help him to find her. Donovan was very impatient. In the meantime, he went to the library to do a lot of research on his own. Big mistake. He had the address of his grandma on some of the paperwork. He took a punt and wrote to that address. Jesus. Far too quickly he found his mother without telling me. He had ignored all the advice from the Social Worker, and I come to that. Donovan and his mother made contact and got in touch with each other very quickly. It all seemed very rushed and disorganised to me, I had a bad feeling about it all. The Social Worker advised us both that it was way too soon to meet, Donovan wouldn't listen. Against the professional's advice and my advice, too, he went ahead to arrange for his mother to come up to Hackness and stay with us. What a stupid thing to do. It was a disaster. She was far from how he had imagined. She was loud, spoke with a heavy London accent and just completely different to the person Donovan had imagined all those years.

Donovan's mother was called Joy. She

was very loud and had a huge character. She completely took over and hit us both with a wall of questions and apologies. As soon as I met her, I did not warm to her. I didn't particularly like her, I felt she was jealous of me, and it was obvious she didn't like me, either. She looked down her long nose at me and made it crystal clear that she didn't want me around. Donovan and Joy were very emotional. Looking back, it was totally the wrong way of going about the meeting. They should have had supervision and guidance from professionals. They were both emotional and impatient, they just went ahead and met. It was a highly charged atmosphere, as Joy was very emotional, she was very tactile with Donovan, she would sit almost on top of him with her back firmly turned in my direction stroking his face with her long witchy fingers and false nails, trying to convince him that she didn't want to give him up. Donovan would be backing away from her, she just kept on getting closer to him. It was weird, almost sexual. Joy told him that he was the result of a one-night stand with an American serviceman, who was in the Navy at the time. She never saw his father after that one night. She explained that at that time she got pregnant there was no room at the house for a baby. She had been packed off to her auntie's place while she was pregnant. Once she had given birth, Joy went to a mother and Baby Home until Donovan was adopted by the Greggs at six weeks' old. Such a very sad story.

Joy said she remembered the day they came to collect him, she was holding him and crying right up until the last minute, when they had to prize him away from her. She kept repeating that she had never wanted to give him up, she had no choice at the time. Donovan felt sorry for her. I did, too. Donovan also still felt rejected by his mother. He was disappointed when he met her. I don't know what he was expecting, but she definitely was not what he expected, he found her too full on and emotional. Time passed by quickly, they didn't see much of each other though they kept in touch by phone and letters. Joy was way too pushy; she wouldn't give him time to breathe and digest everything she'd told him. She seemed desperate to justify what she had done, but it didn't seem to mean anything to Donovan, he withdrew completely from her after a while and eventually they broke contact even though she was relentless and determined to keep in touch Donovan had made his mind up. She was a disappointment. We didn't really go out as much when we had the flat, we didn't have much money, though we were happy at that time just to stay home and cook. One night, Donovan invited Steve, his lifelong friend, round to our place. They had been friends since primary school, they knew each other very well, even though they hadn't seen each other for a while. He told me Steve was coming over with Amy, his girlfriend. When they arrived, we realised that Amy and I already knew each other, though we had never spoken. When I was at college, we would catch the same bus every morning. We had stood at the same bus shelter and just smiled at each other, she had a great, big, smile. We'd never actually talked, I thought she was really pretty and had a friendly face. I would have liked to have known her more, I just didn't have the confidence at the time to start a conversation and neither did she.

When Steve turned up with Amy, I was delighted. We all hit it off immediately, instantly becoming firm friends. We devoted all our weekends to Steve and Amy, and likewise. We used to see each other alternate weekends at each other's flats. We would play Trivial Pursuit, bake bread and have pate and salad with it, we'd drink cheap wine and, at one point, Steve and Donovan thought it would be a laugh to make their own home brew. They could never wait for it to ferment; they'd end up drinking it while it was still bubbling! Steve was a very heavy drinker; he could drink for England. Donovan struggled to keep up though he managed it. We had such great fun together. One Saturday we were just about to have our pate and bread feast at the kitchen table when we found a massive slug trail on the kitchen floor. Steve and Donovan thought it would be hilarious to have a slug race. They found 2 huge white slugs near the sink and lined them up, they were vile. They spent ages pushing the slugs along, eventually they got bored, gave up and slung them both out into the garden. They were like a pair of naughty kids. It was good to see Donovan having fun even though it was slightly cruel.

One year, we decided to go on holiday to France for a week. We didn't have a lot of spare cash; we couldn't afford new clothes. Amy offered to make some holiday outfits for us on her sewing machine. She would call me over after work for a fitting. She did a fabulous job, we thought we were the bees' knees in our home-made skirts and tops, which were all elasticated waists and square shaped! When we arrived at the resort, we were gutted to find the room dirty, and the place seemed like it was under construction. Typical! We had been ripped off. We decided to make the best of it, with the help of copious amounts of cheap wine, we survived. Next thing, we all got the runs, we were running to the toilet constantly, the gripes were very painful, as usual though we managed to see the funny side, it was hilarious. After dozens of trips to the one and only bathroom, we started to applaud each other when one of us bragged that they'd passed a firm stool! Towards the end of the week, we decided to go to the beach together for the day. We were having a lovely time, enjoying a few beers in the sun, when without warning Donovan turned nasty in front of Steve and Amy. I had bought him a watch for his birthday. Suddenly, he took a dislike to it, grabbed hold of me tightly, as he ripped the watch off his wrist, then he tried to push it down my throat! It was totally bizarre behaviour, which came from nowhere, no warning signs. He really hurt me. Steve and Amy were both shocked, they found his behaviour really uncomfortable. Feeling really embarrassed they went back to the hotel room, leaving me and Donovan at the beach. He really scared me; he'd never been physically violent before with me. I was mortified but felt really stupid at the same time. I even thought it was all my fault for getting him a watch he didn't like. It happened at the end of our holiday, and it soured everything for all of us. We came back in silence on the plane.

We didn't see much of Steve and Amy after that incident, I think they did not want to be involved with us anymore. Whenever we tried to arrange to meet up with them, they kept making excuses that they had stuff to do. Eventually, we got the message, we stopped contacting them. It was sad to lose them, we had been so close, I missed Amy very much, she had become like a sister to me, but I totally understood why they didn't want to see us. I blamed myself for wrecking our friendship and so did Donovan of course.

CHAPTER 5

Our Own Home 1980

In the months that followed, Donovan didn't show any more signs of physical violence towards me, though he still belittled me in company, he seemed to be getting more and more intolerant and critical of me. I felt like an irritation to him. Like an itch he couldn't scratch. Consequently, I became very withdrawn. I was always very careful with what I said, I felt I had to think hard before I opened my mouth, in case I said the wrong thing.

We didn't see much of our families. My Mum and Dad were doing their own thing really, going off on coach trips and to the seaside together, they seemed to be getting on better than ever. My Dad didn't like Donovan from the word go. He never used to speak to him, or try to have a conversation, the feeling was mutual as Donovan made no effort with Dad either. My parents didn't come round to visit very often, I didn't invite them to be honest, as I never really felt comfortable. I was always worried that Donovan would start to belittle me in front of them. I didn't want them to know he did that. I was embarrassed. I spoke to them on the phone to keep in touch, though I never told them anything about Donovan's dominating behaviour. Actually, I didn't have to tell them, they knew what he was like, even if I tried to hide it.

My sister fell in love around this time. When Dina met Paddy, she fell for him, hook, line and sinker. As soon as she clapped eyes on him. He asked her to move in with him and his parents at their home in Hackness. She became pregnant not long after and as Paddy's family were all staunch Catholics, it was assumed that Dina would go through with the pregnancy. They started to plan their wedding and put their names down on the Council house list in Hackness. My Mum made Dina's wedding dress and I was going to be a bridesmaid, wearing a bright green silk dress. I was very proud to be Dina's only bridesmaid. Donovan and I didn't see much of Dina and Paddy either. Again, they didn't really get on with Donovan, there was no effort on either side. My brother, Harry, was working at the Post Office in those days. He'd been transferred to another bigger office, where he was working in the post coding department. He was doing really well and had worked his way up from the counter, told you he was clever!

After a while Harry moved into a flat. I didn't see him very often at all, though I was always pleased to see him. He had his troubles I think but he seemed happy enough. He was very close with my Mum and would visit regularly. We all had our own lives, but we knew we were all there for each other if we needed to be.

Dina worked at a local fruit stall in an arcade of shops in Hackness, she seemed happy enough and kept working there until she had their first baby, Donal. Dina and Paddy were still living with Paddy's parents, until they got their Council house in Hackness. Paddy was working as a panel beater at that time. One day, he became seriously ill and ended up on a ventilator with pneumonia, I remember it being touch and go for a few days. Dina was beside herself, she adored him. He came through it. Back at home, he decided he would give up the panel beating as the fumes from the garage and dust affected him, instead he would train to be a teacher.

Dina and Paddy supported the Labour Party, and they campaigned for the local MP in their spare time. They had little money though seemed so happy, Dina baking quiches and flapjacks, like they were going out of fashion, and cooking lentils constantly. She was such a good cook. Seemed like she could whip up a meal from nothing in minutes. They had a big garden and made part of it into a vegetable plot, they lived off their own produce. They were like hippies, Dina was beautiful with her long, blonde hair, no makeup, and Paddy with his big, whacky, curly, black hair. Dina became pregnant again, they had a daughter, they named her Emma. Their family seemed complete. A quirky, little, self-sufficient, family. They had very little materially, yet they were so happy together, making their own entertainment, spending lots of time in their garden. Later on, Dina decided to join Paddy to become a teacher herself, she started a teacher training course, juggling the kids and the training. My Mum and Paddy's Mum helped out with the kids for them while they both went to college.

After a couple of years at the flat, Donovan and I decided to buy a house together. The first house we saw was a three bedroomed, terrace house, in Hackness. Donovan really liked it straightaway, I wanted to look around a bit to see what else was out there. He wouldn't do that and decided to put an offer in straightaway. They were asking £20,500 for it; we gave them the asking price. We got a hundred percent mortgage, as we didn't have any savings for a deposit. Despite it being the first house, we saw, and I had wanted to look around a bit further, we were very excited to have our own place. We moved in as soon as we could. I remember the moving in day was a bit of a disappointment. The couple that had lived there before us, left it in a right state, it was filthy, they had a dog and it had obviously been shut up in one of the small bedrooms upstairs, as there were dried up piles of dog shit still in there, it stank. I was gutted, it was not what I had expected at all. I was very disappointed. Donovan just laughed it off, leaving me to clean the house top to toe, while he fiddled about trying to build the furniture. He was not the handiest person, there would always be a screw left over at the end of the building exercise. He always seemed to be in a rush to get things done, he didn't really take pride in the way he did things. The decoration in our new home was very dated, there was wood chip wallpaper everywhere from floor to ceiling. It reminded me of rice pudding. It was quite a dark house, too. I loved it though, it was to be our family home, or at least that was what I had hoped for.

Donovan left the optical place; he became a postman. He worked early shifts and was either on foot, or he rode his bike. Due to the hours, he started to go to bed about 8pm. He always got up way too early. He didn't start work until 5:30am, yet he would get up about 3:30am. A creature of habit, Donovan liked to follow his strict little routines. He would eat the same breakfast every day, at the same time. He would work until around 2pm in the afternoon, come home and then he'd have a sleep. Later, he'd get up for a couple of hours to have tea, then return to bed. He seemed to be getting much more sleep than me. We started to join in with the social events at the Post Office. There were loads of postmen our age group, who all had wives or girlfriends, the social scene was pretty good. We used to meet just about every Saturday night at the local Working Men's Club. There would be a huge group of us, the women would all congregate together, and the men would sit near the bar. Donovan was becoming very possessive. He didn't like me to be away from him for too long. Whenever I looked over in his direction, I'd catch him watching me, he started to look quite scary and just stared at me, until I got uncomfortable and looked away. I really enjoyed meeting up with the other girls, I became good friends with two or three of them. I wasn't interested, in the slightest, in any of the postmen, though I would chat to them if they chatted to me, only out of politeness, nothing more.

Donovan had a couple of friends that he liked to spent time with, in particular, sometimes on a Sunday at the local football matches. He was not interested in playing sport or anything to do with keeping fit, though he wanted to be involved. He became the Treasurer for the Post Office Football Team. It made him feel important, he would spend a lot of his spare time watching the matches and supporting the team. I was pleased for him that he had found something he enjoyed. This meant that I had most Sunday mornings to myself, I used to put Madonna on full blast and clean the house, dancing around the room, feeling free to be me.

Donovan was always into old fashioned music like Louis Armstrong. It was fun to play the music I preferred; I enjoyed my Sunday mornings dance sessions. Sometimes Donovan's friends would come back to our house with him for a cup of tea and a chat after the games. I would always make them their tea and disappear to busy myself either upstairs, or in another room, away from them. I thought nothing of it. As far as I was concerned, they were talking football and work, I was in the way.

We started having weekly dinner parties with two or three other couples and we all took turns to host them in our own homes. Bit like the telly show Come Dine With Me. It was great fun, I enjoyed creating the menu and trying new dishes. One night, I made a curry crumble that I had seen on some television show, and I thought it looked a bit different, I made it, to try it out on Donovan. He looked at it with total disgust and said, "What is this shit?"

Before I could answer him, he had thrown it all over the walls in the dining room, plate and all. I was so shocked, I just said it was 'a curry crumble'. Donovan came right up to my face and through his gritted teeth, he said, "I am not eating that shit, make me something else."

I did and I apologised about fifty times. I was scared, somehow, he made me feel like it was a stupid thing to make, and it was my fault that he wouldn't eat it.

Donovan was still the same in company, though any chance he got, he seemed to be putting me down. People started to notice, the girls, in particular. Time passed and life continued. Inevitably, as happens when there are groups of men and women, we started arranging for the girls to go out separately from the men sometimes. Donovan was not keen at all on these nights out. I wanted to go though, I felt if I didn't that, I would be left out of the girls group. I stuck to my guns and went along.

One night, Donovan was getting ready to go out with the men, I was getting ready to go out with the girls and I'd bought some really nice pink silk, floaty, trousers. I know they sound awful now, back then, they were all the rage, I loved them. I was really looking forward to wearing them with a pink blouse. They were a bargain from a local quirky shop, I loved a bargain.

I had literally just put them on, when Donovan came into the bedroom, he stopped in his tracks, looked at me, and said, "You're not wearing those, are you?"

I replied, "Yes, I am, why?"

He snapped, "Oh no, you're not, you look ridiculous, take them off."
He looked furious.

I said, a bit nervously, "But I really like them."
Donovan ignored what I said and came over to me.

85

He told me, "Take them off and wear something else, you are not going out in those you look like a fucking clown."

I was scared, I knew he meant what he said. I took them off and put them on the bed. I was upset and I didn't want him to see me crying, I went downstairs for a minute. When I composed myself, I returned to the bedroom. I couldn't believe what I saw, he had cut up my lovely new trousers into ribbons, which he'd put all over the bed. I was extremely upset; I couldn't believe that he would do that. Why? What's wrong with him. He had been drinking Jack Daniels, while we were getting ready. I heard him go downstairs and he was drinking with two of the girls that I was going out with, they had come round to get a taxi all together. It was obvious to both the girls that there had been a problem, I came downstairs with a pair of suitable trousers on instead. I felt dull and boring compared to my flamboyant pink trousers.

Donovan just looked at me and said, "That's better."

The girls looked at me, they knew something wasn't right. I was sure they were wondering about what he'd done. As soon as we got into the taxi, they asked me what had happened. I was reluctant to tell them, as I didn't want them to think bad of Donovan, or me for letting him speak to me like that. I was really upset that he had cut them up, I just told them what had happened, they were stunned though not surprised, they had guessed that he had a bit of a possessive side to him. They had no idea though, that he was a bully, as well! It took me a while to get over that, eventually I did and although I didn't forget it, I moved on and put it behind us, thinking it would be a one off. How wrong could I have been.

After about a year in our own home, we decided to get engaged. Donovan chose an engagement ring out of my Mum's Grattan catalogue and paid for it weekly. I was over the moon; I couldn't believe that he wanted to actually marry me. Me! I was so happy. I thought this is what we needed to do, it would make things better, give us both more security. A part of me thought maybe Donovan's possessive behaviour was due to him being insecure, and he thought I was going to leave him, that was why he was possessive, a strange way of thinking I know, though that's what I believed. Anyway, I don't think Mum and Dad were very pleased that we had decided to get engaged, particularly Dad, though they went along with it, accepting that it was what I wanted more than anything. I was well on the way to my goal. I just wanted to make Donovan happy, at last.

It wasn't long before Donovan started talking about getting married and how we were going to do it. I was still quite shy to speak of what I wanted, though I would have loved a proper church wedding with all the trimmings, I knew that we couldn't afford it. As it wasn't what Donovan wanted, it was never going to happen. He didn't really want any of his family there either. He decided that it would be best if neither of our families were there, then nobody would feel left out. This was not what I wanted at all, I felt terrible. I didn't want to hurt Mum and Dad by not inviting them. What could I do? I couldn't invite them, if we were not going to invite Donovan's Dad and his second wife, Elana. What a dilemma. I agonised over it for hours. Deep down I knew that I had no choice. I had to do as Donovan decreed. It was decided that Donovan would book the Register Office, we would get a couple of witnesses, and after the wedding, we would tell our families. I was so unhappy about this, I knew it would destroy my Mum in particular, she would be very hurt. I couldn't argue with Donovan, it would be like poking a bear and who would do that! I had to go along with his plans.

He booked the Register Office for the 16 August. I set about finding something to wear. I ended up buying a purple dress with black lines through it, like a cocktail type of dress, nothing special really, it was about £20 from New Look. I bought a black hat with a ribbon on it and some maroon shoes and a matching bag. Looking back, they were hideous choices.

That is what happened. Where was the joy? The trips to the wedding shops sipping champagne with my friends. None of that. Donovan was all set, he had his brown suit, the one he was wearing when we met, that would do for him, no need to buy anything special, after all it was only our wedding day! Anyway, the build-up to the wedding was awful. Instead of being excited and happy, I constantly felt very bad over not telling all of our families, I couldn't speak to any of them in case I let it slip. It was bittersweet, on the one hand I was over the moon to be marrying the man of my dreams and, on the other, I knew it would cause emotional carnage with our families, and, in particular, with mine.

I did the right thing, just what I had to do, and I went ahead with it. I was a total bag of nerves on the day, when we turned up at the Register Office together and we had decided that Dina and Paddy could be the witnesses. I was so pleased to have them there. Although I was astounded to see Donovan's father turn up outside the Register Office. Anyway, we did it, we got married, at last I became Mrs Donovan Gregg. lucky me! After the wedding, we went for a meal at a local pub. Later, we went home, got changed and as we had arranged to go to Donovan's Grandma's home down South for a few days, we had to catch the bus from the station, mid-afternoon. I was elated and happy and so very sad, all at the same time. It was such a hard day for me. Donovan was just pleased that we had got it over with and we were finally married. Mission accomplished. He had me. We went to the bus station and had boarded our bus and sat down. We were waiting to leave for our journey. I turned to look out of the window. To my horror, there stood my Mum! My whole body shook, I was mortified, she had come to wave us off, how did she know, who told her, what do I do? As all these questions spun around my head, I just wanted to run off the bus and throw myself into her arms. Mum had a hanky in her hand and looked like she was crying. I couldn't speak, I just nudged Donovan with my elbow and pointed at Mum out of the window.

Donovan said, waving at her, "Ah, there she is."

I was so confused, I looked at him and said, "How do you think she knew we would be on this bus?"

He stared at me with stone cold eyes and said, "I don't know, Dina must have told her we would be here after the wedding this morning." Blaming my sister!! Bloody hell. How dare he?

At that, the bus pulled out of the station, and I just burst into floods of tears as we left, I turned to wave, Mum had gone.

CHAPTER 6

Fatherhood and Babies 1985

We talked about having kids from the word go, though we didn't really think about it seriously for a couple of years. I changed my job again and went to work in an insurance underwriter, where I transcribed site visits for accidents in factories, like Ross Foods. As I found the work fascinating, the time just flew by. It wasn't the sort of place where people could chat all the time, hence I was quiet most of the time. The bulk of our work consisted of audio typing, we all wore headphones, which wasn't conducive to talk with other staff. I have to say though it suited me, as I just wanted to get on with the job. I actually became a very fast typist, at last I found something I was good at! Life continued as usual, Donovan was still content with being a postman, we still saw friends, had our dinner parties and attended post office social events. Emotionally, I still felt unhappy due to Donovan's constant monitoring and watching my every move. He longed to have children more than anything, he'd say he wanted something he could call his own and with his blood. Perhaps this was Donovan's way of compensating for his own childhood and being given away when as a baby. I know he struggled with the adoption issue all the time back then. We decided to have our first baby.

In hardly any time at all, I started to feel really queasy and tired. Then, when I missed a period, which was just not like me, I knew I was pregnant even before I went to see the doctor. I was excited when I went into the surgery and over the moon when the doctor confirmed I was pregnant. I felt so clever, I just knew this was going to make Donovan ecstatic! I was happy to give him the child that he'd wanted for ages. I was overjoyed for Donovan, finally he was going to have something of his own, a blood relative, his own child. I was pleased for myself, too, of course, it's just my focus had always been on my husband's wants and needs, I just wanted him to be fulfilled. This was the icing on the cake for him. I hurried home to tell Donovan. He was still at work when I got home, I sat in the lounge in a sort of daze, I was elated, yet fearful at the same time. I was growing a person inside of me and, one way or another, it was going to have to come out! That terrified me at the time. It was a strange feeling. Fortunately, I didn't experience any vomiting sessions during the first months of my pregnancy. I've always hated throwing up with a passion, it's one of my worst fears. I felt queasy constantly though, mostly in the evenings which was odd, trust me to get that wrong, too! When Donovan came home, I burst through the lounge door into the kitchen excited to tell him. He cried. At last, some real emotion. I was so happy.

I carried on working in the underwriter's office until I was about seven months' pregnant, when I decided to leave. I hadn't been there long enough to get maternity pay and as the management were being awkward about me taking time off for appointments, I decided it was easier to leave when I did. I just wanted to get out of there, I didn't intend to go back to work fulltime after the baby was born either. I was absolutely amazed when, at fourteen weeks, the baby moved. We didn't know what the baby's sex was at the time, as we didn't want to know, preferring to be surprised. I felt that so long as it was a baby, I was happy!

I kept having weird dreams that my baby would be born with no eyes, or really long, alien-like, fingers. I think it was caused by my anxiety. I couldn't take my eyes off my tummy when it moved around, it absolutely fascinated me, and it felt amazing. I'd watch as the baby would stretch across my tummy, suddenly an elbow or knee would float across my skin, then pop back into place. It was indescribable. I felt so clever, growing another person. I tried involving Donovan as much as possible. He just didn't seem that interested, he quickly became bored with me telling him to come here and look at our baby moving around. I was overjoyed with excitement, desperate to share it with him, though you could guarantee when he did finally come over to look, the baby would stop moving just as Donovan sat down. I don't think he believed me half the time, he would just sigh, get up again, and walk away. He seemed bored with the whole pregnancy thing. Or maybe jealous that he wasn't carrying our baby... I don't know.

After a while Donovan got bored with me twittering on, he would just ignore my excitement. I got the message; I gave up trying to involve him. It was only my pleasure, I just kept it to myself. It seemed to me as if he was becoming more and more irritated by my squeals of delight and my joy when I talked to my bump. I started to think Donovan was jealous of his own baby. After all, this is something only I could do for him. In his eyes, I was becoming a mother and we knew how he felt about them, as both his mothers had let him down, his opinion of them was extremely low. I was worried I was falling into the same category with them. Surely not. I was carrying his baby and I was his wife, which must be a different story?

I didn't know anyone else who was pregnant, until one day my next-door neighbour suggested I meet Carol, one of her work colleagues, who was at the same stage as me. They came home together one lunchtime and, as soon as I met

Carol, we hit it off instantly. We kept in touch regularly throughout our pregnancies, swapping aches, pains and worries, generally we had a moan with each other. It really helped to know someone else, who felt the same things as me and it was all 'normal'. Carol was to become a great friend later on and a very important person in my life. She was incredibly kind, such a lovely soul. Carol seemed very together about her pregnancy as she just got on with it. She was a natural mother completely. It came very easy to her. Things became more strained between Donovan and me. He didn't seem interested in me at all. He just worked, slept, ate, slept, worked, rinse and repeat. He became quite argumentative about stuff, even on the TV, I just felt like a complete and utter irritation to him. He still didn't show much interest in the baby bump.

One evening, when Donovan was having a soak in the bath, I was just sitting on the toilet, not using it, chit chatting away to him. The toilet was situated behind the bath, he had his back to me. One minute we were talking away about something, nothing earth shattering, the next minute Donovan jumped up on to his feet in a flying rage. He turned to face me, cupped his hands and threw the bath water all over me. Where the hell did that come from? What had I said or done? Extremely shocked, I felt sick. I was drenched from top to toe. I froze up completely and could only look at him. Donovan didn't say a word, just stood there staring back at me. I was worried that the shock would harm the baby, I grabbed a towel, rushing into our bedroom to dry myself off. I could not believe my husband would do such a thing to me, when I was carrying his child. I didn't know what I had done wrong, either. I can only assume from his behaviour that he was jealous that I could carry the child that he wanted so badly. I felt like he was turning against me, and I was just the vessel to give him what he really wanted, a baby. After that outburst, I completely withdrew, keeping as quiet as I could. I didn't want to make things worse; I felt the best thing to do was to keep quiet and try not to rattle his cage. That was difficult as half the time when he lashed out, it seemed to be for no reason at all. I never knew when he would blow.

As this was to be my first baby, naturally I was pretty scared of giving birth, and as the due date loomed, I began to feel totally alone. I couldn't tell anyone about Donovan's behaviour, I was too ashamed. The bad dreams continued. I would wake up in a cold sweat, believing what I had dreamt about. I had those kind of dreams many times, right up until the birth. *Coronation Street*, a popular English soap opera series on tv, was just about to start, when I felt a ping inside my stomach and had griping pains. The baby was due on the 5th of November 1985, and it was now the 4th. I had felt mega tired and sick all day and a bit strange, though I just put it down to nerves and the constant tension in the house. I didn't know what to expect, consequently I was on high alert. Donovan had been at work as usual; I had spent most of the day watching my bump. It wasn't moving quite as much as before, though I think that was down to lack of space in there as the baby would be fully grown by now.

I was terrified that this thing had to come out of me somehow. I had no idea how the hell I was going to get something the size of a space hopper out of me. Anyway, the pains got worse, I couldn't settle. We rang the hospital, they suggested that we came into the labour suite. Typically, when we got there, of course, everything stopped. The nurses abruptly said that nothing was happening and sent Donovan home. They said they would keep me in for observation, though it didn't seem likely that anything was going to happen overnight. I stayed in the hospital and was put on the maternity ward. It was a relief in a way to be away from the tension.

The midwife told me that I was in the very early stages of labour, it was probably going to be a long time before anything would happen, she recommended I try to get some sleep. I didn't think there was a hope in hell that I would sleep, I was really scared. I woke up around 3am,

I was lying on my back, something went pop inside me, and the bed was suddenly soaked with a yellow liquid like water. I panicked, calling for the nurse.

Calmly, she came over, "It's ok, your waters just broke."

I didn't know what that meant. Nobody had told me anything about what to expect. We had no Google then, probably a good thing in my case. I really wanted Donovan to be with me now. The nurse told me there was no need to contact him as it would be a long time before anything happened. How did she know? I asked her if she had children, to which she replied, no, she hadn't! I trusted her advice though, she and another nurse cleaned my bed up, placing a pad on me, she told me to go back to sleep. As if! There was no chance I could sleep. After that it seemed like two nights rolled into one, time dragged by until daylight. I didn't have any pains or any sign of movement apart from the plug thing which came out, it looked like one of the slugs Donovan and Steve had tormented that time in the flat!

Early in the next morning, the nurse rang Donovan, he came down to the hospital to sit with me. The contractions didn't really start until late morning, when they became thick and fast. I was petrified. I couldn't imagine how I was going to get this great big lump out of me and survive. By about 2pm, I felt extremely uncomfortable, I just could not settle into one position. I tried walking up and down the ward, I lay on my back, my side, my knees crouched down. You name it, I tried it. Nothing I tried helped at all, it was unbearable. I didn't know where to put myself. I was sucking away at the pethidine mask; however, it did not touch the pain. Eventually, I got the urge to push, once that started, I just wanted to get this baby out. We didn't know if our child was to be a boy or a girl at that time, consequently, we couldn't wait to meet him or her. Much endless pushing, shoving, screaming and swearing, later, Tyler was born. He weighed in at 9lb 2 oz. I was exhausted. That boy took some pushing out, apparently, he had a big head! You're telling me, it was literally like passing a fully blown space hopper out of me! What a relief!

As soon as Tyler was born, the nurses weighed him, wiped him down, handing him over to Donovan first, as I was unable to hold our boy yet. I had to wait for the doctor to come and give me some stitches, I needed them due to being cut to facilitate the birth. I was aching to see Tyler, just to hold him close to my heart. Donovan moved away with our child and sat down at the side of the room. I could not even see Tyler from where I was lying on the bed. Donovan was crying. I was happy for my husband, it was amazing. It was as if I'd given him all his birthday and Christmas presents in one go. He looked elated with happiness, clearly, he fell in love with Tyler straightaway. It was a while before the doctor arrived to stitch me up. I just lay there, watching Donovan and Tyler together, it was beautiful. I felt full of joy, not to mention glad that I was still alive and had survived the ordeal!

Tyler was born on 5 November, Bonfire Night. By the time they had cleaned me up, the fireworks had started. I was transferred to the maternity ward, which was situated across the car park in some temporary huts as the hospital was having some renovations. The nurses wrapped me up in silver foil, put Tyler in my arms, then wheeled us across the car park. I felt like a jacket potato in the foil! It was really magical, though, as we were crossed the car park, fireworks were going off above our heads, lighting up the sky, almost as if they were celebrating Tyler's arrival in this world! It was perfect. I was euphoric, relieved that I had our baby, at last. Donovan came with us to the ward and as soon as we got there, he took Tyler from me, sitting next to the bed holding him. He couldn't take his eyes off his son. I'd never seen Donovan as happy as he was now. I felt complete, though completely exhausted. The nurse came with some toast and tea for me, then it was time for me to try and feed Tyler. Donovan decided to leave and left me alone to try to breast feed our son, as he didn't seem comfortable enough to stay and support me with that. He told me he'd go and wet the baby's head with some friends, which was fine with me. I wanted some time alone with Tyler. My baby was just so lovely, with his shock of black hair, which the nurses explained caused the heartburn I'd suffered with during the pregnancy.

The next day Tyler and I were moved to a smaller cottage hospital in Hackness, a wonderful place for new mums and their babies. There were about eight of us. It depended on which GP you were registered with, if you got lucky, you'd be taken there following the birth. I was one of the lucky ones. What a lovely place, it was like a great big old house with low beams, it had nooks and crannies all over the place. The nurses were excellent, all very kind and helpful. They would bring afternoon tea on a silver tray for us and every evening they would take the babies away and give us a glass of Guinness to drink. Within seconds we would be pissed, as we sat around an open fire. I could have stayed there forever with Tyler! The nurses taught us how to bath our babies. One day, they bathed Tyler to show the others how to do it and he behaved really well, he was such a quiet baby, he hardly made a sound. I adored him.

The nurses seemed to have all the time in the world for us, knowing that we were all first time Mums, and we didn't have a clue as to what we were doing. I loved it; I was there for the maximum stay of ten days. Not bad for the NHS. I didn't want to go home. After my ten days was up, I did go home, it was such a strange feeling. The overwhelming feeling was the responsibility I now felt for this small, fragile, little person, that Donovan and I had made. I couldn't think about it too much, as I would get anxious about whether we would be able to do things right for our son. I became really aware of world events, as I was worried for the future. I had a feeling of dread, maybe it was just post-natal depression. The house seemed different, cold and dark. I was worried Tyler wouldn't be warm enough.

Donovan helped with Tyler as much as he could, he never seemed to want to put him down, I didn't get much cuddle time with Tyler, as whenever he wasn't feeding or sleeping, Donovan seemed to be carrying him around. I didn't get a look in, apart from feeding time. I breastfed my baby, it was really enjoyable. Donovan was trying to encourage me to put him on a bottle to allow him to feed Tyler, too. I didn't do that, though, as I wanted to feed my son myself. I knew that if I gave in and let Donovan bottle feed him, he wouldn't let me have him at all, as he could do everything for Tyler, and I would become surplus to requirements. Time went by very quickly and I was recovering from the birth fast, too.

One day, I decided I needed to start exercising. Donovan had a friend at work called Taffy, who had run the New York Marathon, he was a keen runner. Donovan mentioned to him that I was thinking of starting to run and arranged for Taffy and me to go for a run together, he could help me to learn and train. We started with running a mile. We would meet up on the road and ran for a mile or so together. It was great, I loved it straight away. We started to meet regularly in the early evenings and as it was winter and dark outside, it was good to have a man to run with. I didn't really want to go out alone to run. As soon as Donovan came in from work, he'd take Tyler and I'd go out running, without feeling that I was missing out on time spent with my son.

After a while, Taffy and I began to run further, obviously this would take us longer. I was out for about an hour, as we'd run for about six miles. I absolutely loved it. Donovan started getting suspicious. He asked me why I had been out for so long. When I told him we had run further, he said he didn't believe me. He must have thought we were having an affair. How wrong could he be, after all, he set this up in the first place. Or was that his plan? Anyway, it all became very difficult, I was sick of Donovan accusing me of things that just weren't happening. I told Taffy I couldn't continue to go running with him. He was pissed off that Donovan would think such things, he was a married man, all we were doing was running together! Donovan and Taffy didn't speak much after that.

I found a local running club for females only and joined, I went every Wednesday evening, other times I'd just go running on my own in the daytime. Sometimes, I felt I had to go out, to avoid Donovan and his controlling ways. It was my time, I needed it. Tyler was such a good baby, we established a regular routine, he would sleep soundly, it was smooth like clockwork. After his bath, I would put Tyler in his bed at 7:30pm, within seconds, he'd be fast asleep. Amazing! A tubby little thing, he was always the one laid flat on his back at play groups, though he was happy and smiling all the time. He didn't crawl or even show any signs of wanting to move, until his first birthday. He shuffled along the floor. Eventually he started to walk, and he and Donovan became inseparable.

Donovan used to take him up to the football on Sunday mornings, he would walk all the way there, with Tyler on his shoulders. Donovan didn't want to put his son down. One day, all three of us were walking through Hackness, Tyler was in the middle of us, we were swinging him between us intermittently and just as we were swinging him Donovan let go of his hand. Tyler flew through the air, landing on his bottom. He was really upset, I rushed over to pick him up and Donovan pushed me out of the way.

He shouted at me, "You stupid thing! Why did you let go of him?"

I didn't let go of our precious son; it was Donovan who let go! I felt terrible, I just took the blame.

After a while we were struggling without my salary. I took a part time job at the local off licence, it was literally just at the end of our road. I worked three nights a week, starting at 6pm until it closed at 11pm. Donovan used to love it, it meant that he had even more time with Tyler by himself. He would bath him, put him to bed, without me around. I hated it, I didn't want to work there, I had to do it as we needed the money. I just got on with it, though I found it tiring and I was shattered all the time. I was also unable to run in the evenings, as I did previously.

Eventually Donovan started saying it would be a good idea for us to have another baby, while Tyler was still young. At first, due to things not being right between us, I thought it would not be wise. He said that it would be good for Tyler to have a sister or a brother, as the younger he was, the less jealous or pushed out he would feel. I agreed with him on that point, though I still had my misgivings about whether it would be good for us as a couple. After a while I began to think it perhaps it would bring us closer together, it would be good for us. Donovan didn't give up until, finally, I agreed that we would have another child, though I insisted that I wasn't ready yet. We were using the cap as a contraceptive and what a carry on that was. Anyway, I thought as long as we were careful, we could continue using it, until we had decided together that the time was right to throw it in the bin and try for another baby. On the other hand, Donovan had other ideas. I started to feel really tired and queasy again, just like when I became pregnant with Tyler. I thought I was just hormonal or something, after all we hadn't agreed to start trying for another baby yet, *or had we?* It became very clear that I was, indeed, pregnant again.

I went to the doctor, it was confirmed. I was shocked and said we'd been using the cap. I was pleased, though I was still not ready. Donovan, in contrast, was more than ready. When I told him I was pregnant, saying that I was shocked and wondered how it could have happened as we had been so careful.

Donovan smiled and said, "Well, you might have been careful, but I wasn't."

I looked at him and asked, "What do you mean?"

He replied, "I made a hole in the cap so it wouldn't work."

I was gobsmacked. Once again, Donovan had made the decision for us. The second pregnancy passed by without incident. I became extremely big very quickly and the weight seemed to go on all over me. I blew up like a balloon. I craved mashed potato sandwiches in white bread. Couldn't get enough of them. I was rapidly running out of clothes. Luckily Donovan's sister had some really nice maternity wear, she gave me several cotton dresses that she didn't intend to use again. They were not my taste, with great big bows around the neckline and huge patterns but I was desperate. They'd already had their family; they had decided not to have any more children. Donovan carried on spending most of his time either at work, asleep, or with Tyler. Once again, Donovan showed very little interest in me or the moving bump. Just like with Tyler, I was amazed by the movement inside me, I'd spend many hours just watching my tummy moving from side to side, backwards and forwards, it was a miracle to me. I was just as fascinated as I was with Tyler's pregnancy. I loved it.

I hoped I was wrong but still got the feeling that Donovan just looked on me as the vessel to make what he really wanted, another child. I was simply there to give him babies. He didn't really pay me much attention as a person, our social life wasn't what it used to be before Tyler arrived either. Perhaps that was a good thing. Donovan wasn't spending as many evenings with his old friend, *Jack Daniels*, meaning I was no longer being subjected to Donovan's overbearing opinions, or getting caught up in debates, due to the influence of alcohol. At least it was a temporary respite for me, for a while.

It was about 5am, when I woke up at home with severe pains, I felt incredibly uncomfortable. We had arranged with our neighbour who lived opposite, that no matter what time of day it was, she would look after Tyler for us if we needed her to do that. Donovan wasn't at work; it was the weekend. I already had my bag packed with the hope of a week's 'holiday', after the birth at the cottage hospital! We rang the hospital, explained my symptoms, they said to come in now. Donovan woke Tyler up, took him over to the neighbour's house. Poor little Tyler was looking a bit bemused and didn't really want to be left with anyone else. We managed to convince him that we wouldn't be long, and we would have a lovely sister or brother for him to meet very soon. My boy was tearful as we left though he was okay, and we knew he'd be well looked after. I didn't like leaving him and neither did Donovan.

When we arrived at the hospital, everything seemed to stop though not for long! Sweet lord, the contractions were coming thick and fast, just like with Tyler's birth, I was sucking on the painkiller mask for dear life. This went on for several hours, it became obvious that there was some problem. The nurse called the duty doctor to take a look. He said that the baby was laying slightly to the side, meaning my waters were unable to break. They had to get permission from my GP to break my waters. I was getting very tired by that point, I just wanted them to get the baby out as quickly as possible and as it was about 2pm in the afternoon now, I'd had more than enough. Unfortunately, my GP had decided to go off wind surfing or doing some bizarre activity, they could not reach him to get the permission they needed. They could see that the baby was starting to get distressed. They decided the best thing to do was to break the waters. After all that unnecessary time and delay, they finally popped the waters and all hell seemed to break loose, it was as if my body had been possessed, I couldn't control it! I had a desperate urge to push, despite them telling me not to, as the baby wasn't positioned correctly. Fuck that! I thought and just started to push for England. Of course, due to the delays and uncertainty about the situation, they'd forgotten to give me any pain relief.

I was in agony and shouting, "Just get the fucking thing out."

Donovan was just sitting beside the bed, he looked totally helpless, though he kept repeating himself and urging me to *hurry up, he needed to get back to pick up Tyler!* As if I could do anything to make this happen quicker! Boom! At 4:20pm, my Sarah burst into the world, she shot out like a bullet. The nurse only just caught her, scooping her up and holding her up above my head. Oh my, she was a sight to behold! Sarah was blue, purple, covered in blood, etc, screaming her head off! She looked really scary! I couldn't help but scream myself! Donovan stood up to take her, though the nurse just looked at him and said, "No, I will pop her on to her mum."

I got to hold Sarah first. Once I got over the shock, I looked at her little face. Wow! She was incredibly beautiful with lots of black hair. She opened her eyes, looked right at me. Sarah had one blue eye, the other was half blue and half brown. I fell in love instantly, again. Donovan shed a couple of tears, then said he was off to collect his son. He was very worried about Tyler, as we didn't leave him with anyone else very often, I think he was just anxious to get back to him. I was simply glad to be alive and have my gorgeous daughter in my arms. After a while, the nurses took Sarah from me, placing her gently in a cot beside my bed. She was extremely quiet as she lay there, playing with her fingers. Meanwhile, the doctor came to give me stitches, just like I had last time with Tyler's birth. Jesus, they didn't numb the area at that time and that was almost as painful as giving birth.

What a magical day it was for me, I got the chance to bond immediately with Sarah, unlike with Tyler, who'd spent the first few hours of his life in Donovan's arms, not mine. I regretted that very much, I still wished I had been stronger at that time and insisted that Tyler was given to me first. I was so elated that Donovan had his wish fulfilled, I'd just put him first, not thinking about how it was really important for a mother to bond with her baby first, before the father. If I had known then what I know now, I would have demanded to hold my baby first – oh, isn't hindsight a wonderful thing? Donovan brought Tyler into the hospital the next day to meet his sweet sister. We had wrapped up a few little presents and put them in her cot telling Tyler that she had brought them with her. That worked! Although he didn't show much interest in Sarah, but he was chuffed with the presents and hopefully he felt involved and not pushed out.

It became apparent that Sarah had been lying like a frog inside me with her knees and the insides of her thighs upwards. She was born with dislocated hips. She seemed to be comfortable, lying on her tummy, though it looked like she had no legs, they were firmly tucked up towards her shoulders. After a couple of months, Sarah was fitted with a plastic brace to try to reset her hips, she wore it for about six months and, thankfully, it worked.

CHAPTER 7

Mystery Stalker and an Unwanted Party 1989

After a while I had returned to my job at the Off Licence down the road. The phone rang in the back office. I was the only person working at the time, it was about 8:30pm. When I picked up the phone there didn't seem to be anyone there, though I could hear and sense something or someone. Nobody spoke. It was very unnerving, it happened on and off a few times, though only when I was on the shift. Nobody else had taken any of these calls on their shifts. The weird thing was it began to happen at home, as well, at different times throughout the day. I told Donovan; he didn't seem bothered at all. I started getting really worried after a while, I began to dread the phone ringing, especially at work. One night, it happened again while I was at work, this time the person spoke to me.

The voice at the other end just said, "I know who you are, Sophia."

I freaked out, asking, "Who are you?"

Clearly it was a man calling, he just kept on

repeating that he knew who I was. I slammed the phone down and went back into the front of the shop, looking out of the window to find out if I could see anyone in the phone box down the road. It was empty, of course, though that fact didn't help in the slightest.

This kept on happening, every time all the caller would say was, "I know who you are Sophia." Until one day, he also added, "And I know where you live, and you have two children."

Well, this was the last straw for me, I'd had enough. I told the manager of the off licence what had been happening and that I'd been receiving these calls at home, too. She immediately reported it to her superior. In turn, they reported it to the police. I became very anxious as I felt that I was being watched constantly by this stranger. Completely freaked out now, I was reluctant to go to work or even to leave my house. Donovan just kept saying I was paranoid, it was nothing to worry about, who would be bothered about me? When the police came to interview me, all I could tell them was that these calls had been happening on and off, both at work and home, over the last two to three months. They were becoming more frequent now, the caller claimed to know who I was and that I had children. I was also concerned about how he had got my home phone number. The police said they would monitor the lines and let me know if they had any news for me. They advised me that if the calls kept happening, I should put the phone down and try not to engage in any conversation. I didn't think that advice was any help whatsoever, frankly, I was terrified. Especially as this man had mentioned my kids.

After a month or so, the calls stopped. The police confirmed the caller had been one of the regular customers who came in the off licence. He'd been watching me and got my name off my name badge with it on, we all wore them at work. This mad had stalked me as I walked from home to work and back again, he had got my home phone number from the telephone directory. I was shocked when I realised who it was, he was an officer from the local army camp, who always seemed really nice and normal! He never seemed particularly odd or different to me. After this traumatic event, I decided to leave the off licence. It worried me and I didn't believe that this man would back off. It was a shame as the job was very handy for me, it wasn't bad money for the hours. I knew I would have to find something else, I started looking for other evening work. I got a job as a care assistant at a local care home in Hackness. Big mistake!

I wasn't cut out for that job at all. It was working on night shifts, the hours were from 8pm until 8am the next day, for two nights over the weekend. I thought that would fit in quite well with the kids and as Donovan's shifts were through the week, it'd be fine for me to work at those times. In those days, we didn't have much of a social life at all, I could work weekends easily. The only problem was that when I came home Donovan seemed to forget that I had been up all night. He went for his usual nap in the afternoon, leaving me struggling to stay awake with the kids. It then took me days to catch up on my sleep, it wasn't ideal. Donovan and I began to spend less and less time together, too, we became like ships passing in the night. The job itself wasn't too bad, the time went by quickly, as most of the residents were up and about overnight, they had no idea what time it was, half of them thought they were either on the farm they used to run or living in their own world as they danced around their rooms. When I first started, I was warned never to accept sweets from one particular lady, she used to keep her Quality Street wrappers and wrap up her own shit in them to make them look like sweets. She would then try and hand them out to the nurses! They also told me not to get too close to her, as she would scrape her nails down the side of your face, trying to scratch you.

I thought it was a nut house, it made me very nervous. I was mostly doing some ironing, preparing breakfast, or trying to get the residents to go back to bed, never a dull moment there.

The end came for me when I was made to see a dead body. A very small elderly lady called Ethel had cancer and she was at the end of her life. I found it very distressing, she was leaping up out of bed and seeing relatives who weren't there, shouting out their names. Ethel seemed to be highly stressed, in terrific pain, extremely anxious, she was scared and looked wild. It just seemed like a struggle to me, I couldn't bear to see her like that. This happened for a couple of shifts. On the third night, I went in, and she had died that day. I was relieved for her that she had been finally allowed to rest. One of the owners of the home asked me if I had seen a dead body. Of course, I hadn't. She encouraged me to go in and see Ethel, telling me that it would be good for me to see Ethel at peace. I would remember her like that, rather than in pain and struggling like she had been before her passing. Well, when I saw Ethel laying on the bed, her face was full of pain and fear, she didn't look anywhere near at peace, I just took one look at her and left the room. It was awful. After that, I decided I definitely wasn't cut out for that job and handed in my notice.

Donovan wasn't happy about it as the weekend overnight hours meant that he got even more time with the kids. I just couldn't keep going there. It was a depressing job; I couldn't do it. Hats off to those who can. I started looking for another evening job and applied to be a receptionist in a taxi office. The hours were more or less the same as the off licence, starting at 6pm though I didn't finish until 12 midnight, if I was lucky. I was also tasked with directing the taxis, too. That was hilarious, as I hadn't got a clue about locations in the area. The drivers used to dread me coming on shift. They would be passing each other as they zig zagged through the town, up and down, in empty cars, going to the next pick up. They used to say is that bloody Sophia on the shift again! They laughed about it, too.

I had no idea of the street names either. How I kept that job only God knows. I think they felt sorry for me as I was trying my best. I worked in a small office with a heavy chain smoker called Karey, she had no teeth and was rough as rats. She was really nice though, she used to order a takeaway every night and one of the drivers would bring her special fried rice into the office. She used to munch away on it, spitting bits of it all over the controller desk and you could hardly see us both through a cloud of thick smoke. I must have smoked more cigarettes than her! Karey would have a fag in her hand most of the time while she was talking on the phone, spitting rice everywhere, or chatting to the drivers in the office. Despite that I liked her and felt I could trust her. Plus, I always got free taxi rides. Bonus!

Donovan and I didn't get much chance

to see friends or family with us both working, juggling the kids and Donovan's voluntary work as the Treasurer with the Post Office football team. I managed to maintain regular contact with Carol though, we would see each other every Tuesday, she would walk to my place with her two kids one week, I would go to hers the next week. Carol had a great way with the children, she used to always manage to get them to settle down and spent hours reading to them. She was such a calm person. I loved to see her; we would have a good old natter while the kids played. I didn't really need to tell her what was going on at home, she knew without me having to say anything. She had guessed. When it was her turn to come to our house, Donovan would crash through the door about 3pm, when he'd finished his shift. He would just say hello to her, then disappear upstairs to bed. He was very anti-social; she knew there was a dominance there. I would really look forward to seeing Carol, come rain or shine, or even thick snow, we would wade through the elements to be able to spend the day together. She had a log fire at her house, it was always burning bright, she also made the best tuna sandwiches, too. Carol had two boys both the same ages as Tyler and Sarah, her husband had his own stonemason business, and he was a wicked cook. He did all the shopping and cooking for their family. He was very quiet and a nice bloke.

They seemed to have a very settled relationship, they understood each other.

Donovan's 30th birthday was coming up in a few months. I thought it would be a good idea to throw him a surprise party at our house. Yet another attempt to make him happy, perhaps I was hoping it would bring us closer together and prove how much I loved him. Wrong again! I spent weeks planning that party with the help of several of our friends. We arranged it for a Saturday night as Donovan would never go out or do anything on a Friday night as he often worked on Saturday mornings and would need to get up at stupid o'clock. I thought that would work really well as he could come home and have a bit of a sleep. We agreed that I should try to get him out of the house between 4pm and 7pm, which would give me the time I needed to get the party food and everything for the party ready.

A couple of the postmen agreed to arrange to take him for a pint, which would keep him away from the house. They would come up with a reason why it had to be early, something to do with babysitters, etc. That would work. Along with the other wives, I arranged to make different dishes at each of our houses, then get it all to our house while the men were out at the pub. It took lots of secret telephone calls and everyone pulling together to make this party happen. I invited all the family and about thirty odd friends to join us. It was going to be such a surprise, I thought Donovan would absolutely love having everyone in the same place at once. Donovan's birthday finally arrived, and everything seemed to be going well. I tried to make some secret food dishes while Donovan was at work and while he was having a nap after work. Afterwards, I woke him up for him to go and meet the lads for a couple of drinks, he wasn't keen on going. God knows how I did it, I managed to persuade him to go along in the end. He told me that he wouldn't be very long as he really didn't feel like it. *Oh shit.* Anyway, as soon as he left, I got both the kids in the bath and ready for bed. They were being very good, and they didn't know anything about the party. I knew they would sleep through an atom bomb; it wouldn't be a problem having them in the house while we all celebrated downstairs. They both fell asleep instantly, they always were really good sleepers. They could sleep through an earthquake!

A couple of wives arrived with their food offerings, and they started to blow up balloons and getting the house all sparkled up. It was very exciting, I just kept thinking how pleased Donovan was going to be. I did it to make him happy, I felt sure it was going to work. Many people started arriving at the house, bringing food and drink with them and presents for Donovan's birthday which I hadn't expected or asked for. As the time ticked on by, I managed to get the kids to bed, then I went upstairs to get ready for the party, leaving everyone downstairs having a drink. I got a phone call from Donovan's sister, Viola, she said she was on her way. She had to stop at a phone box to call me though to let me know she had started to throw up after leaving the house, and she couldn't stop. Viola was very posh, she was absolutely mortified that she had been on the side of the road throwing up and as people drove past her, they were all waving and cheering, they thought she was drunk! That tickled me.

Viola went on to say that she would be with us as soon as she could, though if she was going to end up turning up at the same time as Donovan, she would hold back in case she gave the game away. I wasn't actually that chuffed she was still coming, I tried to put her off as we didn't want to catch whatever bugs she had! Anyway, Viola was hell bent on coming, I couldn't refuse her entry! I carried on getting ready. I had bought a red velvet, fitted dress, which was off the shoulder and fitted. I'd lost all my baby weight, I felt like a million dollars, I had some red lippy to go with it and red shoes. I wanted to look special for Donovan on his 30th birthday party. I felt great. I went downstairs, the time was whizzing by, I topped up everyone with booze and a party popper or balloon in hand. We were all now waiting, with bated breath, for the birthday boy to arrive. Ten minutes later, the front door opened. Everyone was quiet, we were all in the dining room.

When Donovan came through the dining room door, he looked absolutely stunned as we all jumped up, shouting, "Surprise, Happy Birthday!"

He was speechless, with delight or so I hoped. He scanned the room and couldn't believe that there were that many people, including his family, packed together in our dining room. At first, he didn't see me. After he had caught his breath, he looked right at me, and I saw his face change. Everyone was giggling as they started to mingle again and topping up their drinks. Donovan came straight over to me and with a fake smile, he grabbed hold of my arm, saying,

"Come into the other room with me."

I could feel his fingers digging into my flesh. It hurt. I followed him into the lounge and stood away from him, waiting for him to say a huge thank you to me for going to all this trouble. How wrong could I have been, he was absolutely furious.

He snapped at me, "What the hell have you done this for?"

In shock, I answered, "I did it for you, I thought you would love it."

Donovan just looked at me with such venom and pure hate in his big brown eyes, as he snarled, through gritted teeth, "If you can lie to me for weeks over this, what else have you been lying to me about?"

With that, he stomped out of the room. He was livid. I was shocked and scared. I was upset as I thought, yet again, I have made a mistake. All I had wanted to do was to make him proud and happy. What the hell do I have to do to make this man happy. I don't think anyone noticed Donovan's disgust, thankfully. By the end of the night, Donovan had drunk so many drinks, he didn't seem to care that much about it. I thought I had got away with it. When the people had all finally left, I started to tidy up. I was dreading what Donovan was going to say. To my surprise, he just came into the kitchen to announce that he was knackered and going up to bed. Thank God, I had got away with it. However, I told myself that was the first and the last time that I would do anything like that for him, that's for sure. Everyone had a great time at the party, it was a big success after all, though I think Donovan thought it was more of a betrayal than a nice thing to do for him. He didn't speak to me afterwards, apart from the odd grunt for a few days. He just couldn't seem to see the good side of me, he was constantly searching for a bad side, which just simply wasn't there. All I ever wanted to do was make him happy. Failed again.

CHAPTER 8

Brushed by Death 1991

As was our usual pattern, we moved on from the party and things settled down again. Donovan and Tyler began to spend a lot of boys' time together, Sarah and I would make the most of those times. I had bought a small trampoline and when Donovan took Tyler out on Sundays, I used to put some disco tunes on and bounce away on the trampoline carrying Sarah, she loved it and used to laugh her head off. It was our time. We had such fun together. Sarah would go to bed for a snooze in the afternoons, the only thing was she didn't sleep, she was very cute. I would put her to bed, give her a teddy and her blanket, she would just lie there good as gold, watching me walk out of the room. When I went back an hour or so later, she would be in the exact same position, eyes wide open and she'd giggle as I went back in the room. She was such a quiet, happy little girl. I absolutely adored her. Tyler was quite reserved most of the time. Apart from when he had a part in the nursery school nativity play, he played a shepherd. I was sitting in the audience with my Mum and Dad. As Tyler came out onto the stage, he was wearing the usual tea towel on his head.

Suddenly, totally oblivious to anyone else in the room, he spotted his grandad sitting next to me and shouted, "Look grandad, I've got a tea towel on my head."

Everyone laughed, Tyler just looked at us all, as if to say, *what's funny?* Of course, his grandad had tears in his eyes, he was so proud.

When Sarah was about 18 months old, I woke up to find blood on my nighty. Where had that come from? I couldn't find a cut or anything, I felt my nose, it wasn't bleeding for a change as I did get random nose bleeds, but that was not it, this time. I got up and went in the shower. Blood started running down my body, it seemed to be coming from my nipple. How strange. Nothing hurt, though I thought I should get it checked out and made an appointment at the doctors. Typically, by the time I got to my appointment, the blood seemed to have dried up and I couldn't see any sign of it. I nearly cancelled the appointment though something told me not to and I went along. I told the doctor what had happened. After he examined me, he said just as a precaution he would refer me to the breast clinic at Hackness Hospital and I would be seen in about two weeks, of course he said do not worry. Impossible! I'd had already decided that I had breast cancer and it was bound to have spread to my other organs. I was doomed and only had weeks to live. When I told Donovan he just dismissed it as me being over cautious, he was sure it would be absolutely nothing at all and I was being paranoid. Why was he so sure? I just needed reassurance, not him being an arse, yet again.

The appointment came through for me to go to the hospital within a couple of days. Donovan said he would come with me. Though, as it turned out, it was during his work shift, and he decided it wasn't worth taking time off. I went on my own. I saw a very abrupt female doctor, who didn't have much of a bedside manner, she was straight to the point. She examined me for lumps and bumps, didn't say much apart from she would book me in for a biopsy.

"What?" I said. "Why? What do you think it is?"

"Well, I don't know, but there is something in there and it will have to come out," she replied, saying it just like that, as if it was nothing!

It was, of course, the last thing I wanted to hear. I was scared, worried and actually quite shocked. She sent me away to wait for the appointment for the biopsy, which came through in record time and before I knew it, I was in hospital. I was absolutely terrified, imagining everything that could go wrong, from being put to sleep and never waking up, to not being here to watch my kids grow up. I was a complete mess. Donovan didn't come with me, he was working. He was convinced that it was all a big fuss over nothing, and he thought that I'd be fine. Naturally, this did not help me at all. Luckily for me, I had a friend at the time called Angie, she was a nurse at the hospital. She was working on a shift when I arrived to be booked in. She was very nice, reassuring me that it was all going to be fine. I didn't believe her. As I lay in bed in the pre-med room, I cried. When I started to lose consciousness, I pleaded with them to tell my kids that I loved them. Just bloody stupid, looking back, though on that day I was totally scared out of my wits. Anyway, the next thing I knew I had survived. I woke up to see my friend was sitting next to my bed, she was holding my hand. She was chewing a mint – I hate mint, it makes me feel sick.

"Hello, it's all over," Angie confirmed, as she gently squeezed my hand.

I felt lousy. The first thing I did was to feel my boobs, checking whether or not they were both intact. Thank God I did that, as I realised one of them was heavily bandaged. I was desperate to know what they had found; however, Angie didn't know. Nobody came to see me until the end of that long day. Finally, the nurse came in to tell me it was okay for me to go home. Donovan came to pick me up, still convinced that this was a huge fuss over nothing, and I would be fine. I was really sore and felt lousy after the anaesthetic. I went straight to bed when I got home, still not knowing what they had found. I was rigid with fear. I couldn't stop thinking I was doomed and convinced myself it would be bad news.

A week later, I returned to get my results. Donovan actually came with me that day. We were waiting ages before they called us in to see the doctor.

Before we had even sat down, the doctor just said, matter-of-factly, "Okay, it was an infected duct and we removed it."
She said it like I should have known that and that I was stupid because I didn't. I thought she was on the verge of being rude, though I was extremely relieved at her words. Then, overwhelmed, I burst into tears. I think both the doctor and Donovan thought I was overreacting. Thank God, I was alright. Cancel the funeral!
When we left the hospital, Donovan turned to me, saying, "Told you."

I couldn't answer him. I just wanted to get home and see the kids. We lived in a terrace house, most of our neighbours were around the same age as us, and their kids were of a similar age as ours, too. The youngsters would all play together on the back street and we mums would take turns to watch them to ensure they were all still there.

We would sit out on dining room chairs, moving from house to house to have tea and chat about nothing. We used to have mini street parties, our next-door neighbour was in charge of the music and we'd all chip in to provide food. Of course, we would share some wine and once the kids went to bed, we would all stay out on the street, drinking until the early hours. It was all such fun, I really enjoyed seeing all the children play together and it was nice all the grown-ups got along well. Donovan was always the first adult to go inside, he just was not very sociable. He didn't really like mixing with our neighbours. I don't think he liked them. Frankly, they sure as hell didn't like him, he was plain rude. Still up to his usual tricks, he would try to make me look and feel stupid. After a couple of glasses of wine, it didn't bother me as much, I used to just laugh it off and ignore him.

Many a time after we'd been enjoying a street party, Donovan would say things like, "Why don't you just fuck off, we don't need you, we would be better off without you!"

I lost count of the number of times he said that to me after he'd been drinking. He knew deep down that I would never leave my kids. That's why he felt safe saying it, he knew he could say anything to me, and I wouldn't go. However, it did take a toll on me and after a while I began to believe that he meant it, he really didn't want me around, after all he had got what he wanted, a boy and a girl of his own. I wasn't needed anymore. Donovan seemed hell bent on getting me to leave. I would never do that. I couldn't leave without the kids. He always said to me that I could never take them from him, as if I did, he would hang himself. I absolutely believed that he would follow through with his threat to commit suicide, one hundred per cent. I was trapped. I would have to just put up with his behaviour and concentrate on the kids. I thought Donovan may get tired of saying the same things after a while and give up. Fat chance.

Donovan decided to change his shifts at the Post Office, as he wanted to deliver post by van, rather than on foot or using a bike. I changed my job, too, as we needed more money. I now had a full-time job in a Solicitors. I worked in the Wills and Probate Department for a really grumpy bloke. A huge, fierce, man, who smoked like a chimney. Everyone was scared of him. He would summon me up to his office, telling me to bring my book. I used to have to sit opposite him, with a cigarette burning in his ash tray right in front of me. He never actually smoked it, though I sure as hell did. I hated it, as my clothes and hair would stink of smoke. I'd be sat there for ages, while he barked orders at me. He would then take phone calls, still insisting that I stay there, waiting for him to finish his call. Despite all of that, I enjoyed the job overall, I actually became quite good at it.

Whilst Donovan and I were out working, Tyler and Sarah were looked after by Lynette, a child minder, who lived opposite us, over the back street. She was really nice and had two children of her own. All the youngsters got on well, plus she was cheaper than most others around there. I'd drop them at her place around 8.15am and she'd take them to school and pick them up in the afternoon, and I'd collect them from her home when I returned from work. Everything seemed to be going well, apart from Donovan's never-ending irritation with me and his constant calls for me to leave.

Any chance he got, he would say, "Just go, we don't fucking need you."

My default was happy, people used to comment on how much I smiled no matter what was going on inside. However, his negative attitude was really starting to get me down. There was no way on earth I was leaving my kids, I would just have to put up with it and hope it would he would eventually stop. Donovan used to get up around 5am. One morning, unusually for me, I had woken up and saw his shadow as he got dressed and I got a strong whiff of his aftershave. It was still dark; we didn't speak to each other. I heard him go downstairs, get his breakfast and the packed lunch I'd made him. A few minutes later, I heard the door go as he left. I fell back to sleep. About an hour later, I woke up again. It was as if a massive flash of lightning or something had lit up the room. I sat up and looked round the room to find the source of the light, it was spooky. I had an awful feeling of dread, something wasn't right, I just didn't know what. I woke the kids up, as usual, to get them both ready for school. We were downstairs, I was just about to leave the house to take them to Lynette's place, when the phone rang, and I just knew something was wrong. I picked up the phone and it was the hospital. Donovan had been in an accident.

They told me he had been in a road traffic accident and had been taken to Hackness Hospital and that I should get myself there as soon as possible. I wasn't surprised, it was as if I already knew. A strange calm came over me, I wanted things to be as normal as they could be, I didn't want to frighten or worry the kids, I decided not to tell them about the call. I needed to know more about what had happened before I could tell them anything. I literally threw the kids at Lynette, immediately rushing off to the hospital and was directed to A&E, where I found Donovan laying on a trolley. He was in a terrible state, crying, he was not making any sense whatsoever. It was clear that his leg was smashed, and he was wearing a neck brace. He told me his back was hurting him, too. I asked if he knew what had happened. He told me that he couldn't remember much really, all he did know was that he was involved in a head on crash. He did remember that he saw bright lights in front of him at around 7am that morning. At that exact time, I had woken up to see the bedroom lit up! Spooky!

I tried to calm him down. He was crying uncontrollably, he just kept saying he couldn't bear it. After a shit load of painkillers and tears the police came to interview Donovan. It became clear that he had been pulling out of a farm onto the main road and, for whatever reason, he'd veered over to the wrong side of the road, though he denied that, of course. A local man of about 25 years old was driving a Fiat Uno quite fast and they'd hit each other in a head on collision. Donovan told us he heard the man screaming so much that he couldn't bear it. As the ambulance man took Donovan past the car, he saw the steering wheel was up against the man's chest and his eyes were out of their sockets. Donovan went on to say it was like something from a horror film. He heard them bring the man into the A&E room next to his, the poor man started screaming in agony and then everything went quiet. The man was taken to intensive care and was severely injured. This haunted Donovan.

I stayed with him all morning. In the afternoon, he had to go into surgery to have his knee reset. It was badly broken, it had to be pinned and basically put back together. Donovan was in agony. I hated to see him in such a state, he looked pathetic. Like a little boy, crying constantly, he couldn't cope at all.

He kept asking about the kids, I reassured him that they were fine, and I would go and pick them up from school while he was in surgery, then I would get someone to babysit while I came back later after his operation. Donovan was taken to surgery, and I left the hospital and went to collect the kids. News travels fast, by the time I got to the school everyone knew about the accident. I reassured the kids that Daddy was okay, he would be staying in hospital just for a couple of days. He was actually in there for two weeks. Sadly, the man who was in the other car didn't survive. Although it had looked like he was going to pull through to start with, he took a turn for the worse and his parents had to decide whether or not to turn off the machine. They turned it off.

Donovan really struggled with that; he was riddled with guilt. It later transpired that when the police studied the road markings, it was clear that Donovan had been on the wrong side of the road. They came to the conclusion that Donovan had been reaching over to the passenger side of the van to get some mail out of the bag that was in the footwell, and the van had drifted over to the other side of the road. The van then smashed head on into the other car that had been coming over the hill. It was indeed Donovan's fault. I knew this would be hard for Donovan to admit. I stood by him to back him up when he said that he wasn't on the wrong side of the road, he was adamant that it was not his fault. Apparently, the lad who died was well known in the village for speeding and Donovan latched onto that fact and told people that everyone in the village had said that it was an accident waiting to happen and that the young man was a lunatic driver. Part of me didn't believe that, though I had to stand by Donovan, he was clearly falling into a deep depression, and I couldn't see how he was going to recover mentally from the shock and guilt. I had to support him, come what may.

When Donovan returned home from the hospital, things were difficult enough, then just to top it all off, there was a knock at the door. When I opened it, there stood an elderly couple. They were well dressed and looked like church goers! They were. It was the other driver's parents. I didn't know what to say. How the hell had they got our address? What did they want? Were they angry? Were they going to crucify Donovan? All these questions ran through my head. I had to protect him. Donovan shouted out, asking me who it was at the door. They somehow slipped passed me in the hallway and walked into the lounge, where Donovan was sitting with his leg up in plaster.

They introduced themselves and showed us both a picture of their only son. Donovan burst into tears. I rushed off to the kitchen to make some tea. The kids were playing on the back street and they both came in when they saw me in the kitchen. It wasn't my turn to sit on guard out the back, one of the other mothers was on duty. Anyway, they both came in to see who had called at the front door. They went into the lounge and the couple asked them their names. It was all very awkward and a bit weird. The couple were being really nice, reassuring Donovan that they forgave him, and he had to get on with his own life for their son's sake, they didn't believe that it was anyone's fault and he had to stop feeling guilty about it and move on for the sake of his own children. They had no other children and they asked if they may take Tyler and Sarah out for tea sometime. I thought to myself absolutely no bloody chance, instead I said that would be nice out loud. Why the hell did I say that!? I can only assume they were still in shock and not thinking clearly, how they could be so forgiving. I didn't get it at all, one thing though is for sure, Donovan had a lucky escape as anyone else might have pressed charges for dangerous driving and be after his balls. Not them.

In the days that followed, Donovan was falling deeper into depression, he couldn't face going out, there was absolutely no chance he was going back to work any time soon. The Post Office had to have an investigation into the accident, which seemed to take months to come to a conclusion. We had numerous appointments with their lawyers in Leathley, who convinced us that Donovan would not be charged, as they could prove that it wasn't his fault. To this day I don't know how they did it, but they did. Donovan was not charged, and the case was closed. He had got away with it, but at a cost. He vowed never to drive a vehicle of any sort again. He was really struggling with his injuries. It was months before he would even think about going back to work. The Post Office were very good to him, he was on full pay, they tried to encourage him to go back to work, assuring him that he would not be expected to drive a vehicle. He would be using a bike or on trolley duties only.

Eventually, he did go back and reduced his hours, supposedly on a temporary basis, to get him back in the swing of things. He worked from 5am until 10am. This, of course, meant that he could spend more time with the kids and push me even further away. This was all part of Donovan's new master plan, of course.

When Donovan went back to work, he remained on painkillers, anti-depressants, cigarettes and a renewed friendship with Mr Jack Daniels once more. What a dangerous mix that was. He had made an appointment to see the doctor, which I thought it was only a routine one. Later, it turned out he had made arrangements to have a vasectomy. That was fine by me, as I had no intention of having any more children with him. I was actually glad he had done it, even though once again he didn't think it was necessary to discuss it with me first. Naturally for Donovan, it was the worst pain anyone had ever had, he made a huge deal of the aftereffects. He got over it after a couple of months and I could rest easy knowing that the rare times we did interact, there wouldn't be any more mistakes.

Donovan's friend, Christian Brown, used to come round to see him while he was off work, and they would spend ages together chatting in the lounge. Christian was a real heavy drinker, and they would drink together. They always ended up talking rubbish, though it kept Donovan busy. Christian seemed to be a good friend to Donovan. Whenever he came around, he was always polite to me, I thought he was a nice bloke, nothing more. Christmas arrived and we decided to go along to the Post Office Christmas Party at the Mill Stones, which was a lovely restaurant out in the country. The Post Office had arranged a bus that would pick us up from the end of our road and drop us off after the bash. It was a chance for us to get out and be a couple together again, after everything we had been through. I was looking forward to it. Donovan was on good form, I thought it was going to be a good outing for us. How wrong could I be.

The coach picked us up and it was already

almost full. Everyone was in high spirits, it was Christmas, we were all off the leash. When we got on the bus, I saw Christian Brown sitting in one of the seats, he was single and was by himself. Donovan and I sat a couple of rows in front of him. He nodded to us when we got on the bus, I smiled back at him. Donovan immediately shot me a filthy look and told me to sit down. I shuffled over to the window seat and kept looking out of the window, I was already in trouble. We started the night with the Christmas dinner, it was really nice. We began to relax and enjoy ourselves. I wasn't a big drinker, I just had some wine with the meal, though Donovan started on the JDs. He seemed to be constantly at the bar throughout the meal, leaving me on my own at the table. I was terrified in case any blokes came over to talk to me. As we were all friends, there shouldn't be anything wrong with that, however, I felt like Donovan was watching my every move. I became very nervous, I tried to stay close with the girls in our group and when everyone got up to dance, I joined in. Donovan was alone, stood over at the bar, he was watching us all dancing. Stone faced.

As I turned round, Christian Brown was stood right behind me, he started to dance with me. I completely panicked. I didn't want to be rude and walk away, I just went along with it. Christian was drunk, he was leaning towards me, and I backed away. He followed me and started telling me that he liked me and why did I put up with Donovan's behaviour. I didn't know what to say to him. How did he know Donovan was an arse? I could see Donovan was becoming angrier by the second, I was fucked. Even though I tried to escape from Christian, he kept on following me. I didn't know where to turn, if I went over to Donovan, I thought he would cause a scene, but if I didn't, he would cause a scene, too. I couldn't win. What the hell do I do. I went to the toilet. Good plan, I thought. I stayed in the toilet for what seemed like ages, trying to work out what to do. One of the girls, Little Eileen, came bursting through the door and told me that the coach had come to take us all home and the bash was finished. Thank God, I thought. I grabbed my coat and went to find my husband praying to God I wasn't in trouble again.

Donovan was walking across the car park to the coach, he grabbed me by the arm and started dragging me towards the coach. I told him to get off, he was digging his fingers into my arm, and it hurt, plus people would see him. He just told me to get on the coach and called me a slag. I was terrified. I got on the coach first and he followed me. As we walked down the aisle, he pushed me from behind. A few people noticed; they just rolled their eyes at him. I wanted to tell them I felt I was in danger, yet I could not. Part of me didn't want anyone to know how he treated me; I was ashamed. I probably deserved it for talking to Christian Brown anyway.

That journey seemed like the shortest one ever. The coach stopped at the end of our road and Donovan got up and stood to the side to allow me to go first down the aisle. He pushed me all the way down the coach. He didn't say anything, apart from 'bye' to everyone we passed. I caught Little Eileen's eye, she just smiled at me, it was a knowing smile. I managed to smile back as if there was nothing wrong. I was shaking.

When we got off the coach, he grabbed me by my hair and dragged me down the street to our front door. My sister Dina was babysitting. I didn't want her to know anything was wrong, I asked him to stop it. He just ignored me, he was furious and opened the door pushing me over the doorstep into the house. Dina was staying overnight, she was still up, sitting in the lounge. We went passed the lounge door and he told me to get upstairs. I went upstairs and into the bedroom. I desperately wanted to stay quiet, I didn't want the kids or Dina to know what was going on. He flew through the bedroom door and pushed me onto the bed. I was trying to get him off me, he started punching the back of my head, as I slithered off the bed and onto the floor at the foot of the bed, he was pounding the back of my head and dragging me around the floor. I fell against the wardrobe; he just wouldn't stop. I was shielding my face and head with my arms as he was punching my ears, they felt like they were on fire. I heard Dina run out the front door, she had gone home.

I was so ashamed. Donovan heard her go and stopped. He went downstairs. I was petrified now, I didn't know what to do, or what to expect when he would come back upstairs. I just took my clothes off and got into bed, closed my eyes and hoped to God he didn't come back, and I woke up safe in the morning. I did, on this occasion. He had slept downstairs.

Next morning, it was Saturday. When I went downstairs, I found that Donovan had gone to work. Thank God, I didn't know what to do or say to him. At least I would have some time to think about how to deal with it. I was in shock. My arms were covered in bruises and the back of my head hurt. I couldn't believe what had happened, that was the first time Donovan was really physically abusive. I didn't know what to do about it. I felt terrible, my head and ears were ringing, I felt dizzy and sick. Before long Dina came to see if I was alright.

Before I could say anything, she said, "I don't care what you did or what you said, you did not deserve that, you need to leave him." I couldn't leave, I couldn't leave the kids.

CHAPTER 9

Mrs Gregg and Mr Nasty 1993

S ome joker wrote, *'Mrs G likes change her colours'*, on the toilet walls at the Post Office. If only they knew what carnage that sentence would cause. Obviously, Christian Brown was nowhere to be seen, certainly, he was not visiting Donovan, who now refused to speak to me since that awful night of the Christmas Party, apart from to say, "I hope you die in your sleep."

He used to say that many times as we got into bed. I would lay there, frozen rigid, afraid to go to sleep, in case he did something to me. After the Christmas Party, I was disgusted with his behaviour, not to mention I was really hurt, both physically and mentally. I couldn't believe that my own husband would do such a thing to me, all over a quite innocent dance. He was supposed love me and protect me, not hurt me. He should have been proud of me and pleased that I was his wife. I wished we had never gone to the bloody party and Christian had kept well away from me, he didn't have a clue what trouble he was going to cause, he was drunk, and I am sure he was just being friendly.

I hardly knew him really, whenever he came to the house, I would just make a cuppa and leave them to it, we probably only ever said 'hello' and 'goodbye' each time we saw each other. In addition, Christian knew I was a married woman and Donovan was his friend.

I thought it was obvious to Donovan how uncomfortable Christian had made me feel when I was backing away from him and trying to dodge his conversation, as usual he seemed to be seeing something entirely different happening. Maybe that's what he wanted, an excuse to lash out. Where the hell had that all come from? When Dina came round the day after, she told me to go to the doctors to get checked out and to put this on record. She was extremely upset at what she had heard, she said it sounded like we were throwing furniture around, the noise was dreadful, she couldn't believe that Donovan would do that to me. She didn't know what to do, in the end she just left as she couldn't bear it. She asked me what the heck he had been doing to me. I couldn't lie, I told her the truth that the noise was me crashing against the wardrobe and huddled at the end of the bed.

Dina was now really angry, upset and worried for me. To calm her nerves down, I told her it was a one off and I was sure it would not happen again. She said it had better not happen again, she was livid. She didn't seem convinced and said she had seen the way he looked at me at times and heard the way he spoke to me. That worried me even more, if she had noticed it, how many other people had? I was even more ashamed of myself, as I continued to think it was all my fault and blamed myself for aggravating him. I should have just walked away from Christian and left him on the dance floor, however I really didn't think it would lead to this result. Who would expect such an outburst?

Dina decided not to tell Paddy, her husband, as he would have got involved and that would only make things a million times worse. Paddy was waiting for an opportunity to have a pop at Donovan. He didn't like him. I made her promise not to tell Mum and Dad. I couldn't bear it if they knew what was going on. Plus, my dad had never liked Donovan. I felt sure he would take the opportunity to have a go at Donovan too, which would only make things worse for me! My parents would only worry about me, I couldn't cope with that, on top of everything else. No, I decided it was better for everyone if they didn't know about it. After all, I thought, it would stop after a while, and he would start being nice to me. Fat chance.

I was reluctant to go to the doctors at first. I decided I would just go to stop Dina badgering me about it. For days after, I felt like I was in a void, I was completely spaced out, my ears were ringing, and I felt sick. Spaced out. The doctor confirmed I had concussion. He asked if I had bumped my head or fallen, I managed to hide the bruises on my arms and legs with my clothes, though it was clear that something bad had happened. I told him I had slipped and fallen downstairs. I am a hundred percent certain the doctor didn't believe me, though he said that I needed to take things easy, and it would pass over the next few days. If it didn't, he advised that I should go back to see him again. He asked me if everything was alright at home. I replied that yes, everything was fine, thanks. He clearly didn't believe me. I could tell by the look on his face. I was just relieved to know that I hadn't burst a blood vessel or something in my head. That's how it felt. When I came back from the doctors, Donovan was home from work.

He asked me where I had been and when I told him, he snapped, "You didn't tell him what happened did you?"

I said, "No, don't worry, I don't want anyone to know about it."

He burst into tears and tried to hug me, he kept repeating how sorry he was and that it would never happen again, he didn't know what came over him – all that bullshit. I thought the easiest thing to do would be to just move on and let it go, part of me wanted to believe him and that it was down to his good friend Mr Daniels, though I knew deep down it wasn't. He had a nasty streak. I didn't want to believe he would hurt me like this. I loved him.

After Donovan stopped blubbing, just when I thought things were okay, we could get through this, he told me, "Oh, by the way, some of the lads have written, *'Mrs Gregg likes to change her colours'*, on the wall in the toilets at work – so how the hell do you think I am supposed to deal with that?"

He got angry again and before I had a chance to answer him, he went over to Tyler, who was sitting on the sofa and said right in his face, "Your mummy's a slag, she dances with other men at parties."

Tyler burst into tears looked at us both and went upstairs to his room. I couldn't believe what I was hearing or seeing, how the hell could he do that to Tyler. He was clearly trying to hurt me, though in fact all he was going to do was screw up Tyler. Maybe that was part of the plan, to turn my own son against me. I was furious and tried to stay calm as I didn't want to poke the bear, I decided to let it go. I didn't want to risk another outburst. I hadn't the strength or the energy to deal with another episode. My head was ringing.

I went towards the door to go upstairs to see Tyler, when Donovan jumped in front of me and said, "Don't you dare, I'll go, he doesn't need you, none of us do, you should just go. just fuck off."

I stood back and let him go past me. Trying not to cry. God knows what he was going to say to Tyler, though I felt that if I went upstairs, the chances were that Donovan will start saying hideous things to Tyler again, in another attempt to hurt me. I was really upset that he would do such a thing to Tyler. God only knows how we would get over this. I just sat downstairs on the sofa, in disbelief that I found myself in this nightmare and hoped to God I would wake up and it had all been a dream. I knew I had to let it all go and just try and keep Donovan calm and do as I was told. The alternative was unthinkable. There was no way I wanted to leave, I wanted to be happily married, we had two lovely kids, why couldn't he just accept that I am a good person and all I want to do is be a good wife and mother. Instead, he was hell bent on proving otherwise and was busy creating scenarios in his head that just did not happen, he made them up to have a go at me, making my life hell and so bad that I would leave home and my kids. No chance. I was not leaving. I couldn't even contemplate leaving the kids. I knew that the price would be too high for me to cope with, either way.

The choices would be that I leave without the kids, which was unthinkable, or I leave and take the kids, then he hangs himself, both scenarios were equally unthinkable. I couldn't do that to the kids. One thing I was sure about was that things had to change. This was not going to end well.

What on earth could I do. I felt completely alone and confused. Nobody knew apart from Dina what had happened that night and that's the way it had to be. I had nobody to talk to, nowhere to turn. I decided I just had to get over it, forgive him and carry on, though I had no clue how this was going to end and with him continuing to tell me to, *'fuck off and die in my sleep'*, it wasn't going to be easy. Sometimes I would wake up during the night to find him staring at me, he would then spit in my face. It was terrifying. The only fact I could cling on to was that Donovan would sometimes experience waves of regret and appeared genuinely sorry for what he had done. I must keep reminding myself about that, trying to see the good side of him for all our sakes. I didn't want the kids upset or disrupted in any way, shape or form. I would do anything to keep them safe and happy. They meant the world to me; I didn't want them hurt. I still loved Donovan, too, despite his behaviour and I wasn't prepared to give it all up. Surely, we could work through it together, couldn't we? Time passed by things seemed to be getting a bit better, Donovan wasn't drinking as much and seemed to be happy with his reduced hours at work. I was working full time; I didn't get as much time as I wanted with the kids during the week. Without realising it at the time we seemed to be swapping roles, Donovan was at home more than me and I became the main earner. This wasn't what I wanted, though it all just seemed to happen like that. Donovan had been through a terrible time after the accident, I just wanted to support him and help him recover, to start enjoying his life again. I kept on making allowances for him and convincing myself that things would improve. I had to believe that. What he had seen on that morning of the accident was horrendous, anyone would be traumatised by that, I kept reminding myself of that, making excuses for his behaviour. He still refused to drive, he was even reluctant to go in the car at all, I ended up doing all the driving.

We didn't go out socially for months after that Christmas, only occasionally we had friend's round. I was always very careful about what I said and kept well away from the men. I would fuss around, topping up drinks, preparing the snacks and food, just trying to avoid any sort of chance that Donovan would kick off again. We didn't see much of my family though that was the usual pattern. Mainly due to me not wanting anyone to guess what was going on. We used to go to see Donovan's Auntie Win, she lived with her friend, Jessie. They had a lovely house, not too far away, and Win seemed to like Donovan, as she often invited us round there on Sundays, she was a heavy smoker with bad asthma. She would suck away on her cigarette, the next minute she'd have a blast on her inhaler! Jessie was the polar opposite of Win, very girly, blonde, curly hair, glamourous, Jessie and I hit it off immediately. She knew what was going on without me having to tell her. She had guessed by some of the things Donovan had said to me when we were round at their house. She would ask me if I was alright and I always said, 'yes, of course', though I know she knew that I was far from alright. It was what we didn't say that spoke volumes and she would just give me a knowing look and told me to let her know if I needed her.

They were members of the local amateur dramatics group, they used to invite us to some of the shows. They were hilarious as Win would overact. She reminded me of Les Dawson, when he used to dress up as a woman. I would chuckle to myself at that. After a while, Win asked us if we would be interested in forming a barber shop quartet. Donovan had a very low singing voice, while Jessie and I had about the same pitch. Donovan had a friend called Al, who had always wanted to be a singer and when Donovan invited him to join, he jumped at the chance of becoming part of it. We used to rehearse at Jessie and Win's house. Win would attempt to direct us while Jessie and I would try to stop laughing long enough to get through the Blue Ridge Mountains of Virginia! We used to crack up at Al's expressions when he sang, it was so funny, I really enjoyed it. We often got told to go and sit on the stairs like a pair of naughty children, until we could compose ourselves enough to stop laughing. We would just look at each other and start giggling, we couldn't help it. For me, it was a chance to escape from the situation at home with Donovan. I felt safe there as I knew that Donovan would not let anything slip in front of Win, he respected her and she was loaded, he wanted to keep on her good side. We did a couple of shows at old people's homes in Hackness, it was really great fun. Jessie and I became very good friends, I trusted her completely. I knew she genuinely cared about me. What I didn't realise at that time was that Win was abusing Jessie and treating her in a similar manner to the way Donovan treated me! It must be something to do with their family! The quartet ran its course after a few months, Al started to make excuses about being unable to rehearse, it sort of fizzled out. It was such fun while it lasted, I felt I had gained a firm friend in Jessie.

Dina didn't want much to do with Donovan after what she witnessed, which meant we didn't see much of her and Paddy either. It felt like we were drifting away from everyone, at least my family anyway. John and Rita worked at the Post Office. John was a really small bloke with ginger hair and small pinched features, he had a real dry sense of humour and was shy yet very funny. Rita was bigger than John, she had mega short hair and from behind you could have mistaken her for a bloke, though she was a lovely person. Rita had been married before and had a daughter, Cath, who was about eighteen and worked in a supermarket. They all lived together at the other side of Hackness.

Donovan and John were quite good friends. I used to chat to Rita when we had been attending the Post Office parties in the past, so I knew her quite well. They were a very well-suited couple; they had such a solid relationship. I envied them for that. They seemed to have such fun together. I think Rita may have been a bit older than John, though it didn't matter. Anyway, we got invited to their wedding, which was in August time. A couple of weeks before the wedding, John had arranged a stag do and Rita had arranged a hen do on the same night. We were invited to both. I was really pleased to have been invited though I was worried, too, as this was the first time, we would have been going out socially since the disastrous night of the Christmas party. Naturally, I was apprehensive.

They arranged that the stags and hens would go to different pubs, to avoid any danger of us all bumping into each other, that's why I thought it would be okay. Rita said there was a chance that we could all meet up at the end of the night at a club, though we would all just wait and see what happened. I hoped not. The night arrived, we arranged for my friend from work Cassie to babysit, she came along with her boyfriend Aidie. They had babysat for us a couple of times before, when we were at Win's house attempting to sing, they already knew the kids very well and Tyler and Sarah liked them. They arrived about 7pm as we were getting ready, they got a drink and played with the kids in the lounge. I was very careful about what clothes I wore, I kept it very low key in order to not to provoke any discussions about my clothes or give Donovan a chance to get his scissors out again!

Donovan went out before me to walk to the local pub and meet the stags there, I was being picked up by a couple of the hens in a cab and heading straight into town. Once Donovan had gone, I started to relax and was looking forward to having some fun with the girls, knowing that Donovan would not be watching me. Or so I thought. We went to a couple of pubs, and everything was going really well. Rita wasn't the sort of person to dress up as a bride, she wouldn't have appreciated a tacky veil, or having willy shaped straws, or blow-up willies, we didn't do any of that stuff. We were just a group of about twenty girls, on a night out, having fun and it was great to be out and about, relaxing with friends. I hadn't felt able to do that for months, I needed it. I had lost myself in all the tension. As Donovan and the stags were out in a different part of town, I was quite confident we wouldn't bump into them, and all would be fine.

By the time we arrived at the third pub, we were all getting a bit tipsy, we were having such fun with each other. We danced our way straight to the bar to order our drinks. I was bursting for a pee and went straight to the toilets, after asking Rita to get my drink for me and I told her I'd get the next one. When I came back to the bar, I went to get my drink from Rita, and we were chatting away. Dancing on the spot to the music. Everything was going well, until I looked over to the other side of the bar, there was Donovan leaning on the counter, he was directly opposite us. My whole body seemed to shake, as the colour drained from my face.

Rita noticed, she asked me, "What on earth is the matter with you, you have gone as white as a sheet, have you seen a ghost?"

I told her that Donovan was at the other side of the bar with his friend, Joey, who was about ten years younger than us. Joey had visited our house, sometimes he'd be on his bike, he would stop for a cup of tea and a chat with Donovan. Rita looked over at Donovan, he was still staring at us. She guessed there was a problem by the look on his face and my reaction. I thought I was seeing things; I couldn't believe that he was there. Rita asked me why I was so stressed about it, I just answered that I was surprised to see him there, as they were not supposed to be going into the same pubs as us.

Rita laughed as she said, "He obviously can't' keep away from you!"

If only she knew. Donovan continued staring at me, I didn't know what to do, whether I should go over to him or not. He seemed to be in a deep conversation with Joey, they both kept looking over at me. When I bit the bullet and went over to Donovan, he clearly didn't really want to talk to me, though he asked me if we were having a good time. I knew he didn't mean it, as he said it in a sarcastic way, with no expression on his face at all. I said yes, we were having a good night. I asked him where the other lads were and if John, Rita's fiancé, would be coming. Rita didn't want to bump into John, as she thought it was bad luck. Donovan said they had got split up in the last pub, Joey and himself had decided to come to this one. He said he had seen us walking in, he just thought he would surprise me. He did that alright.

I offered to get him a drink, he said, "No, it's okay, you get back to your hens."

Donovan grabbed me by the arm as I was moving away, he told me to behave myself. He seemed angry and agitated again. I said I was happy to stay with him if he wanted me to and he told me to go back to the girls.

As I walked away, I heard him say, "I will be watching you."

I was uncomfortable and conscious that Donovan was indeed watching me. We decided to move onto the next bar, I just waved at Donovan as we left. I was very glad to be out of that tense situation, I hoped that we wouldn't bump into them again. Donovan did not turn up at the next bar, I calmed down a bit but was constantly on edge looking at the door in case he appeared. As time was cracking on, and Rita wanted to go to the club, we decided to go straight there. It was now kicking out time at the pubs and the queues were forming outside the clubs. We joined the queue for the club and soon we were in there at the bar. It wasn't very busy when we got in, though within fifteen minutes it started to fill up. We managed to find an empty round table in the corner, where we sat down and started yapping away.

The DJ put Whitney Houston "*I Wanna Dance with* Someone" on, we all jumped up to go and dance. We threw our handbags in to the middle of our circle on the dance floor as tradition dictates! We were dancing the night away, when I became aware of someone watching me again. The smoke machine around the floor was making it difficult to see, it was also quite dark. Suddenly, I noticed a man leaning on the bar who looked like Donovan. I thought I was seeing things and it was my paranoia. It wasn't. I shuddered. He had zero expression on his face. Just a stone-cold stare. There was tap on my shoulder and I turned around. It was young Joey; the bloke Donovan had been with at the bar earlier. He asked if he could dance with me. I panicked and was mortified. I immediately looked back over at Donovan. He had moved away from the bar. Where was he?

Quickly I replied, "No, it's fine, I'm okay on my own."

I tried to turn back, away from him. I was terrified now, in case Donovan had seen Joey talking to me.

Joey wouldn't go away and said, "It's okay, Donovan told me to come over and dance with you, he doesn't mind."

I thought that was weird, though Joey convinced me that Donovan was fine with it. I kept a distance between us and tried to get further and further away from him. Rita was dancing too; she could see I was edgy. She pointed towards the toilets, beckoning me to go with her, thank God, it was a way out of the situation. I picked up my bag, to follow her. She asked me what was going on. I told her I didn't really know, it was all a bit weird, and she said she was worried about me, as she could see that Donovan was staring at me all the time and looked like he was going to explode. She told me she knew what he was like, she had guessed that he wasn't treating me very well. She could read the signs. She asked me outright if he had been hurting me. I finally admitted it to her, she told me that she had been in an abusive marriage, she knew exactly how things could get. I told her that Donovan had told young Joey to come over to dance with me, which I thought was strange. She said he must be setting you up. What the fuck. Why the hell would he do that. I was scared, I didn't know how to get out of the situation without making matters worse, I was starting to get really nervous about going home. Rita told me to stay at her place, she said we will get a taxi together. We went back into the club; Donovan was back in position standing at the bar. Rita told me to keep things as normal as possible, not to worry because she would be watching me.

I went over to stand with Donovan. He didn't say a word. We stood there for a while not saying anything. Eventually he told me he was going to the toilet and would be back in a minute. While he was in the toilet young Joey came over to talk to me again. He asked if I was alright and that he thought Donovan was acting a bit weird. Jesus Christ. I just wanted him to go away. I didn't want to be rude to him, though I was now really scared that Donovan would see us talking when he came back from the toilet, he would get the wrong end of the stick. I told Joey everything was fine and that it would be best if he wasn't seen talking to me when

Donovan came back. Too late. I turned around to see Donovan stood behind me. He was furious. He started calling me a slag and a tart. Everyone turned around, as he started to push me and told me to get my coat, I was coming home with him right now. I was terrified. I knew what would happen if I left with him. I didn't know what to do. Rita came over, she stood in between us, desperately trying to calm Donovan down. She told him to go home and said that she would make sure I got a taxi in a while, but he should go home first to calm himself down. She said she wasn't going to let me go home with him. The secret was out, everyone could see the kind of man I had been living with. I was shaking, terrified about what was to come. The bouncers came over and asked Donovan to leave. He left and I burst into tears. I told Rita I was now scared to go home, and I let her know what he had done to me after the Christmas Party. Rita was really upset for me, she told me I was welcome to go home with her, though it would probably make things worse. It would be wise if we waited a while and gave him time to calm down. Hopefully, Donovan would go straight to sleep when he got home, and I could sneak in the house without waking him up.

We stayed at the club for a while longer, until we thought it would be safe for me to go home. Even though Rita lived at the other end of town, we got a taxi together and she promised me that I would be okay, and he would have gone to sleep by now. She advised me to just go in quietly and get into bed, and to try not to wake him up. Everything would be okay, and she asked me to let her know I was alright, if I could, the next day.

I managed to get through the front door without making too much noise, I took my shoes off and went upstairs to check on the kids, they were both fast asleep thank God. I went in the bedroom and Donovan was already in bed. It looked like he was asleep, too. I got my nightie on and quietly slithered into bed, desperately trying not to move the bed or the quilt as I didn't want to wake him up. I lay on my back, breathing a sigh of relief. I had done it, I was fine. I turned over facing away from Donovan. Within seconds, Donovan jumped up, snapped the bedside light on. He started pushing me out of the bed. I was shocked. I didn't have time to grab hold of the bed, I fell on the floor, he started to punch me, and I put my hands up to protect myself. He dragged me along the floor by my legs and was spitting at me, calling me a slag and a tart, asking me where I had been. I couldn't speak, I was petrified. Donovan was not going to listen to me. He was totally out of control. He started pulling my hair and punching my back. I curled up into a ball to protect myself. I just wanted it to stop. He wouldn't, it was relentless. After what seemed like hours of this, he opened the bedroom door and went downstairs. I was freezing cold, I scrambled back on to the bed and under the quilt, I was praying that he wouldn't come back upstairs, desperately I tried to keep quiet, in case one of the kids woke up.

I did not dare to take even one breath, as I held my breath under the quilt. I desperately didn't want to wake the kids. I didn't want them to see what was going on. I couldn't escape. There was no way out of the house apart from going downstairs. Everything went quiet, I thought he must have fallen asleep downstairs. I was wrong. I didn't hear him creep back upstairs, he burst back in the bedroom through the door, he had a bucket full of cold water and threw it all over me, it was freezing cold! He drenched me from top to toe, the bed was soaked. I just lay there on my back as he climbed on top of me and got right in my face, spitting at me.

Donovan said, "I want you out of here, today, we don't need you, we don't love you, you need to leave today, just fuck off."

By that time, it was about 5am, I was exhausted, I had hardly slept. I felt bruised, broken and I was frightened and full of fear. I was covered in bruises, freezing cold from being soaked and just wanted this to end. I didn't want the kids to know what had happened, I was really distressed and upset. Donovan went downstairs into the kitchen, I heard the kettle, he was making a cup of tea as if nothing had happened. My imagination took over, I was worried he was going to come back with a knife or scald me with the water from the kettle. God only knew what he was capable of. I decided to get up, grabbed some clothes, got dressed and crept downstairs. I went into the dining room to get the car keys, I thought it would be a good idea for me to go out for a couple of hours until he had calmed down and the kids had got up. I could go back to try and talk to him later. Perhaps some time apart would make him realise that he didn't really want me to leave. I searched the room until I realised that he had hidden my car keys. I didn't want to keep searching for them in case it provoked another attack. I got my coat, quietly I left the house. I didn't even take my handbag as I knew I would be going back. I had no choice, I had to get out just for a while. I was broken. I couldn't take it anymore. I thought if I could get away for a couple of hours, he would calm down and change his mind, everything would be okay, he didn't really want me to leave, surely. I walked and walked. I felt terrible, every bone in my body ached, I felt sick. I had that feeling of being in a bottle again. I was sure that I must have been concussed, I'd lost count of the number of times he had hit me on the back of my head. I couldn't believe this was happening. I didn't even know where I was going. After a couple of hours, I found myself at

John and Rita's house on the other side of town. I hesitated before I knocked on the door. Rita opened it as I collapsed in floods of tears. She had been expecting me.

CHAPTER 10

Leaving My Kids Behind 1994

Rita made a cup of tea, we sat at the kitchen table and John joined us. I couldn't stop crying and wasn't making much sense, I was jabbering on. I couldn't think straight, and it felt as if I was watching myself, this was all a dream. A very bad dream. I hoped to God I would wake up soon. I just wanted to see the kids as I was really worried about what they would think, or what Donovan would tell them about where I was that day. I was always there when they woke up, I just could not bear the thought of them wondering where I was or what had happened. They would be upset and confused. I felt really guilty about that, I even felt guilty if I didn't feel guilty. I had no strength left. So many things were going through my head. Not to mention my banging headache from all the blows I had taken.

Totally emotionally exhausted, all I wanted to do was to cry it all away. John didn't know what to say, though he was an excellent listener. He told me not to worry as he knew exactly what Donovan was like, he wasn't surprised that things had gone this far. He had seen signs of his character by the way he behaved at work with other people. I spent most of that day at their kitchen table crying on and off. Just when I had managed to pull myself together, I would start blubbing again. I just couldn't stop crying. The phone rang about 3pm, it was Donovan. Rita picked up and he told her that he'd rung just about everyone we knew, however, nobody knew where I was, and he was getting worried. He asked if either of them had seen or heard from me. Rita responded that they hadn't seen me at all. She asked why and if everything was ok. Donovan, of course, lied, saying we had had a bit of a tiff, though everything was fine, and he was sure I'd be back home soon. Rita was disgusted, she could see I was in bits, covered in bruises, Donovan just referred to it as a "tiff". Unbelievable. As the day went on, we talked and talked, and I was feeling more and more scared about going home. I didn't know what to do. I was so torn. I missed the kids desperately; I was still worried about what they had been told. I didn't want them to be upset. They must have been asking Donovan where I was all day, I was worried about what he may have told them both. Every time I thought about them both I cried. They must have missed me, and they must be asking him questions.

Rita was amazing. She talked to me for hours, I told her everything. She kept saying there was no way I should stay with him, though she totally understood that I didn't want to leave the kids. Rita tried to get me to eat. I couldn't take a bite, I felt like I would choke if I did. I couldn't even think straight. What should I do? If I went back, it may happen again or even worse. As the hours went by, I became more and more anxious about going home. I didn't know what to expect. I hoped that Donovan would be sorry, and it would all blow over. Perhaps we could be a happy family. I knew deep down that was not realistic. He wasn't going to change. He was getting worse. Rita kept saying to me that she would drive me home if I wanted, though she was feeling very worried about what might happen. I just didn't know what to do. I wanted to see the kids to reassure them that everything was okay. The phone rang again at about 4.30pm. It was Donovan again. He was still trying to track me down. John answered the phone this time, he told him that they hadn't seen me and didn't know where I was. I asked them to say that as I needed more time to think about what to do. I was shaking as they spoke to him. This was an impossible situation for me, I just couldn't make a decision. I wasn't thinking straight. I was hurt, upset and physically hurt.

My body ached. Rita made up a camp bed in Cath's bedroom, she said I could stay the night and we would talk again in the morning when things may be a bit clearer. I borrowed Cath's pyjamas. I was so tired and emotionally drained that I fell straight to sleep.

The feeling when I woke up the next morning was awful. I didn't know where I was for a moment. Suddenly, it all came flooding back to me and I just burst into tears again. It was a nightmare. A living hell. All I could think about was my kids, their lovely little faces, I really needed to know if they were alright. My heart ached for them both. John and Rita were both on early shifts and had left for work. I went downstairs and sat with Cath. She was a nice girl, quiet, but a good listener. I don't think she had a clue what to say to me, she just put the MTV music channel on the television. I remember doing fine until a song called 'November Rain' came on when I started to cry again. This just kept happening on and off, one minute I would be composed and thinking that I could get through this, the next one I would be in absolute bits, this went on until John and Rita came home from work. Cath had got used to it, she kept handing me tissues when she saw another tearful outburst brewing. The phone had rung out a couple of times during the morning, Cath said John had told her not to answer it, in case it was Donovan. I started to feel sorry for my husband, it must be difficult for him explaining where I was to the kids. Immediately, I had another thought that he deserved it all, after what he had done. So many mixed feelings were swamping me. I was a complete mess.

We all talked again around the kitchen table, drinking copious amounts of tea. I had such a dread about going home and the same thing happening all over again. Yet, all I wanted was to be back with my kids. Rita suggested that it may be a good idea to log the attack with the police. At first, I was horrified and told her I couldn't do that, it made it real. After a while though, I thought she may be right, just in case it happened again. I decided I'd do it as I needed to protect myself and the kids. Rita drove me to the police station. It was extremely difficult; I didn't want anyone to know about what Donovan had done. Part of me was making excuses for him and more or less trying to convince myself that he didn't really mean it and that I'd deserved it, somehow it must have been my fault. I provoked him. I was petrified. If Donovan found out I'd seen the police, it may even make things worse for me. Anyway, it was too late, as I was sitting in the waiting room at the police station with Rita, then we were called through to go into a little room. I couldn't speak, the words just wouldn't come to me. I couldn't say it out loud, I didn't want it to be real.

Rita spoke for me, telling the police officer what had happened. He was very nice, which made it worse for me, I just couldn't stop crying. They made us both a cup of tea. Eventually, I calmed down, and the police officer asked me to make a statement, just for the records. He explained that if I wanted to press charges for assault, I could do that. What? I couldn't even consider doing that. It didn't make sense to me, I wasn't a battered wife, Donovan loved me. What a load of tosh. I was still trying hard to convince myself that everything was fine, we would get over it. I believed that we wouldn't stand a chance if I pressed charges. The police officer was very firm. He told me that what Donovan had done was not acceptable and if I wanted them to, they could take me home, arrest Donovan for assault and take him into custody, while I got back into the house with my kids. They would then make sure that Donovan would not be able to come near the house, he would be served with a Restraining Order. Holy shit, this was like something off the telly. It couldn't be real. This isn't happening. What a dilemma. I couldn't believe they were talking about me and Donovan. I stumbled over my words; I couldn't decide what to do. The police officer seemed to think it was a no brainer, Donovan had attacked me, and I needed to make him pay for that, as well as get back with my kids.

If only it was that simple. How could I admit that? I couldn't process any of it. They asked whether Donovan was a risk to the children. I replied that he was absolutely not, he would never ever hurt them, it was only me that was at risk. The kids meant the world to us both and *they were his life*. He would never do anything to them. Finally, after about fifty cups of tea, I told them I couldn't ask them to arrest Donovan, as he had always said to me that if ever, I took the kids from him, he would kill himself and I believed him a hundred percent. Donovan would no doubt carry through his threat to end his life. I couldn't live with that. Not for my sake or his, but for the sake of our kids. How would I ever explain it to them, it could screw them both up for life, they might hate me for it. I had to make the hardest choice of my life and decide what to do, I either think of Donovan's wellbeing and mental health, and leave him in the house with the kids or I have him arrested for assaulting me and I go back into the house with my kids. However, the risk of him committing suicide and the kids growing up without a father was not what I wanted, despite what he had done to me, mostly I didn't want my kids to have to deal with that or live with it. The other choice was unthinkable but real. I would have to live my life without my children. Impossible. What the hell do I do? All the options were unbearable. I needed more time to think about it. The police officer told me that nine times out of ten, people who threaten suicide do not actually go through with it. It could turn out to be an empty threat. It was totally my decision, he said.

I was totally convinced that Donovan would

be the one percent that would go through with it. He would. I knew he would. My head was mashed. The policeman told me that they were happy to take me to the house and arrest Donovan. I had to make a decision. While I was trying to decide what to do, they took me to another room and took photographs for their records of my arms, legs and back. Once that had been done, they needed my decision. I asked them to take me to the house to get some clothes, as I hadn't taken anything when I'd left the day before. After all, I hadn't planned to leave. I wasn't prepared, this was not premeditated, I just thought I was going out for a couple of hours, this was unexpected. How was I to know I was going to be so scared to go back into the house. I never expected to feel like this, though I was now beyond terrified of Donovan.

We got into the police car; Rita came with us. The policemen assured me that Donovan would not be allowed by them to go anywhere near me. I was absolutely aching to see my kids, hold them both, to tell them everything was going to be okay though, at the same time, I didn't know if I had the strength to see them. I needed to; I just didn't have the emotional strength. What if they were upset, and asked me not to leave? I couldn't cope with that, even though I was desperate to see them, I knew it would be better if I didn't, both for them and for me. It was very painful. It was after 7:30pm when we pulled up at the house, I was pretty sure the kids would be asleep by now, I just wanted to get into the house, grab some clothes and get out again. I would think about what to do after that. I didn't want to see or talk to Donovan. The police officer knocked on the door and we stood behind him. Donovan answered the door, he looked shocked. He saw me standing behind the police officer, then his eyes filled up with tears. He just stood to one side to let us into the house. He actually looked scared.

The police officer asked Donovan to go into the lounge and stay there. He told him I had just come for some clothes, and I did not want to speak to him. Donovan ignored the copper and tried to talk to me, I just froze completely. I managed to run past the lounge up the stairs into the bedroom, I grabbed any clothes I could, and Rita shoved them into a bin liner. How had it come to this? I didn't like being in the house as I had flashbacks to that awful night when he'd being dragged me around the floor, I just needed to get out of there as quickly as I could. The airing cupboard was in Tyler's bedroom, I needed to get some underwear out of there.

As I crept passed Sarah's room, it was really hard to stop myself from going in to see her, it was nearly impossible to hold myself back, yet I knew I couldn't go in there. I just had to get my things and go as quickly as I could for all our sakes. I opened Tyler's bedroom door and almost crawled in, I hardly dared to breathe, in case he woke up. I was rummaging around in the airing cupboard.

Just when I thought I had got away with it, I heard Tyler's gorgeous voice, saying, "Mum, you're back!"

I turned and saw him sitting bolt upright in his bed, with a beaming smile on his face, as he started to get out of bed. I completely froze, what could I say, what do I do. I was crying.
I just looked at him and said, "No, no Tyler, I'm sorry, I'm not.. I can't ..."

Choking, my throat tightened, I just had to get out, though all I wanted to do was hold him and tell him everything would be alright. I knew it wasn't and I couldn't. I had to go. For his dad's sake, I had to go. I left the room, and I could hear Tyler crying. It was unbearable. I ran down the hallway and down the stairs, dropping knickers on the way, I ran out of the house and fell into the back of the police car. Rita said she would go back and get the bits I had dropped. My heart was totally broken. Tyler was still crying as I left the house, I will never ever forget that, nor will I ever forgive myself for it. He was so delighted to see me. I crushed him by leaving. How do I deal with that? I just fell apart again. Thank God Sarah was asleep and knew nothing about my visit. I hope. I did it for Donovan. I knew he would kill himself if I had got him arrested and I couldn't do that to him. That was a high price for me to pay, though I felt that I had no choice. He would have killed himself without a doubt. It was clear there was no going back. I tried to start thinking about what I was going to do next. I hadn't a clue. Donovan was gathering his troops, within a few days he had turned up at my Mum and Dad's house with the kids, he was crying, saying he had told me to fuck off loads of times, but he never expected that I would actually go! Unbelievable.

Cassie had been the babysitter the night he attacked me. She later told me that she had seen him a few days after when she called round to see if the kids were okay. Donovan told her that it was a good job I had left, otherwise next time he would have got a knife and stabbed me. She knew he wasn't joking; she didn't know what to say to him in response. She told me he was scary, she believed that he would have done it. After a day or two, I plucked up the courage to speak to my Mum. She was clearly upset when she heard about me leaving and was angry with me, as she couldn't understand how I could leave my kids. She told me about Donovan's visit to them with the kids, telling me that he was very upset. Of course, she had no clue about the real reasons that I had not been able to go back home. I told her what he had been doing. Eventually, she began to understand my side of the situation. Donovan's tale was much different to mine. It would be, wouldn't it? I explained to Mum that I had absolutely no choice but to leave the kids. I didn't want them to be dragged from B&B to B&B with me, I wanted them to stay in their own beds with all their toys and in their own house, I didn't want their lives to be disrupted. Mum couldn't understand why I had chosen to leave Donovan in the house. I had to explain that I was worried that Donovan would kill himself. I don't think she believed he would do it, though I think she understood that it was too much of a risk for me. She said Donovan wanted me to go back home. I told her I was too frightened of him, I simply couldn't risk him attacking me again, the next time he did it I may not be so lucky. If that's what I was! I certainly didn't feel lucky, I had lost everything. My kids, my home and my marriage. What else could I lose. I had nothing left.

John and Rita's Wedding Day came, I didn't know whether to go or not. They said it was totally up to me, they understood if I didn't feel up to seeing everyone. I wanted to go to be a part of the wedding, I didn't think anyone would be that bothered about me or my life, I didn't think it would be a problem for me to go. It was a register office wedding ceremony; it was low key, and I managed to get through the service. However, when it came to the night party, things were not that easy for me. After the drink had been flowing, a few people started making sly comments, just loud enough for me to hear. They were saying things such as, *what sort of mother leaves their kids* and calling me a slapper or a tart, under their breath. I could hear them muttering as I walked past them. I couldn't believe it. What did they know about it? I had no choice! What the hell had Donovan told them? I was extremely upset, I just made my excuses and left.

John and Rita were going away for a few days. Before they left, they knew I was desperate to have some time with my kids. I had tried to speak with them, though Donovan was refusing to put either of them on the phone. He said they were too upset, it would just make them worse. It broke my heart every time he refused. One day, Donovan agreed that Rita could pick them up and bring them to see me for an afternoon. I was over the moon. I couldn't wait to get my hands on them both. Sarah didn't seem to have a clue what was going on, she just sat on my knee and was more or less acting normal. Tyler on the other hand was very quiet. I knew he was hurt; he didn't seem to want to talk to me. He just played with John on the street. He seemed to have completely clammed up and if I tried to talk to him, he would just not reply. It was so hard to see him like that. I just wanted to make things better, though I didn't know how. I knew I couldn't go back to Donovan. He was dangerous, I didn't trust him anymore. I couldn't explain that to the kids. I didn't want to admit that Donovan had hurt me, he was their father and I respected that. I didn't want them to be scared of him either.

After about four weeks, I decided to go back to work, I was still sleeping on the camp bed, and I think Cath was getting a bit fed up with me being in her bedroom. It was time for me to pick myself up and start moving on. I went back to work, and all was fine, except Donovan kept turning up with the kids. My desk was in the main window, and he would turn up out of the blue with the kids, just standing across the road as he looked in the window at me. I fell apart every time he did it. My boss started getting angry about it, until one day he went out and asked Donovan to stop doing it, as it was upsetting me and the children. Donovan didn't do it again.

I tried to keep seeing the kids every couple of weeks, just for the day or the afternoon, I couldn't have them overnight, I had nowhere to take them. Sometimes I would ring to confirm I was having them, and Donovan would say they didn't want to see me. I found out later that he had been saying the exact opposite to the kids and telling them that I had rung to say that I didn't want to see them. They would be sitting there all ready and looking forward to seeing me, then he would crush them both by saying I didn't want to see them, this was really wrong of him to do. I was devastated, thinking that they didn't want to see me. They felt the same as he'd told them I did not want to see them! Donovan was evil and playing emotional games with all of us. I had seen Joey a few times. He had popped by after work with John. We became good friends, and he sometimes came with me on days out with the kids. He was really good with them, and they liked him.

Rita always said I could stay with them for as long as I needed, however, I knew it was getting difficult and it was very good of Cath to share her bedroom with me. I now felt the time had arrived for me to move out. I saw an advert for a flat share in the local paper and went to look at the room. The owner was a lovely girl called Ellie. She was some sort of scientist. The room was lovely. It was a big double room, I thought it would be ideal. I got on well with Ellie. She was quite a serious girl and clearly very intelligent. I thought it would work really well as when I went to look at the place, she was fine about me bringing the kids round. I trusted that it wouldn't be a problem and that's why I took the room. I moved in very quickly after that, I felt like I was finally taking control of my life. Ellie was always making homemade soup, though she never gave me any! She was very firm about my cupboard space, and everything was always kept very separate. I did not dare to use her side of the fridge. The first couple of times the kids came to the flat, Ellie was really friendly and nice to them, though after that she seemed to change, saying she'd prefer it if I didn't bring them to the flat, they were noisy and made a mess. Of course, they did, they were kids for God's sake! I was gutted as this meant I had nowhere to take them, I started having to drag them around the valley gardens or get the bus up to Mum and Dad's house. Not ideal.

It was hard filling the time, yet I really looked forward to seeing them and was always in floods of tears every time I dropped them back off at home. Walking away from the house was hell. It was like living with constant grief, I missed them very much and wanted to be with them all the time, even though I knew that was impossible. I wanted to be there at bedtime, bath them, have 'normal' time with them. I lived at Ellie's for six months. One day she came home from work and announced out of the blue that she was moving to America; she had got a job in some amazing laboratory. I was gobsmacked, Ellie hadn't told me she was even thinking of moving, never mind going to America, of all places. I asked her if I could keep the flat on for her and rent it from her myself, she said no, she wouldn't want me to do that. No real explanation either, I guess my time with her was up and it was time to move on again. I felt gutted and lonely. I hadn't seen much of Joey after I moved in with Ellie, she didn't seem to approve of our friendship. Him being 10 years younger than me etc. I didn't see the problem; he was just a friend. We drifted apart after a while. It was a shame because he was always such fun.

As luck would have it, I was on my lunch break a few days later and just wandering around through town when I bumped into Amy! I was really pleased to see her, she gave me a massive hug and said she had heard about Donovan and I splitting up. She was relieved as she always knew what he had been doing and was glad I had got away from him, though she was sorry it cost me the kids. When I told her my current situation, she told me that Jackie, her sister, was looking for a lodger. Amy promised to have a word with her to see if I could go and look at the room. I was delighted. I knew Jackie, though not as well as I knew Amy, I liked her though and thought it would help her out, as well as it would be good for me to be back in touch with Amy again. For the first time since leaving the kids, I felt optimistic.

The following Friday I went to look at Jackie's flat and the room after work. Amy had told me that Jackie was renovating the flat, though she felt sure that the room would be ready quite soon. Jackie opened the door with a beaming smile. She was such a happy, bubbly person, always smiling, face full of freckles and very pretty, with long curly hair. She was an aerobics teacher and did several classes a week, also working as a temporary secretary. She was lovely. We hit it off immediately. It was a top floor flat, we climbed up the stairs. Jackie was hilariously funny; she had such a wicked sense of humour. She showed me the lounge, which was really nice, she had finished that room, then we had a quick look at her room, it just had a mattress on the floor, though no bed yet. She quickly showed me the bathroom, it was half tiled and not quite finished. Finally, she opened the door to my bedroom. It was full of wood, rubbish, you name it, you couldn't see the room for stuff! Jackie just laughed and said, "– and this is your room!" I looked at her as if she was joking, she clearly wasn't. We both laughed. She assured me that the room would at least have a bed in it by the time I moved in. I don't know how she did it, but she managed to get the room ready for me to move into it a week later.

Amy and Steve had split up. She was now with Mike; he had a roofing company and was helping Jackie decorate the flat. Mike had worked day and night to get the room ready for me, they were all really lovely. I really liked being around them. They were always laughing, everything felt like it would be fine when I was with them. From the moment I moved in with Jackie, we did not stop laughing. Although she obviously knew I was still very upset about my situation, she had the knack of making me forget about it for a while, to just enjoy myself. I often felt guilty as if I shouldn't be happy, as I was not with my kids, which feeling kept hitting me like a train. Friday nights were always fun. We would come home from work, open a cheap bottle of wine, Jackie would put her boom box in the hallway, and we would dance away to Dina Carroll, while we got ready to go out with the girls. We used to stumble down the road to the nearby pub, later working our way along the stray visiting other pubs and finally into town. We would finish the evening off at our local nightclub. After dancing, we'd get the obligatory chips and gravy as we wandered back home again. This was our itinerary, most Friday nights.

Jackie would go out with her boyfriend on Saturdays, sometimes she stayed over at his place, and I could have the kids round on Saturdays. I still didn't have them to stay over though, there wasn't really enough room. Donovan wasn't keen for me to have them overnight anyway, he always refused whenever I asked. Jackie's boyfriend was a policeman and he'd often drive a big police van when he was on duty. One night, we were all out and giggling from one bar to the next, when he pulled up beside us, telling us to get in the back, we all piled in, pretending that we'd been arrested, and he drove us to the next bar. We all fell out of the van right outside of the pub. He just drove off, it was hilarious. I enjoyed our crazy nights out and we had a ball most weekends. Another time, we had all been out when I'd found myself locked in the toilets at the club. Somehow, I managed to get out, just before it closed. I had to climb over the top of the toilet door, God knows how I did that!

One of the girls was called Denny, she was really petite. She reminded me of a Beverley Sister with short hair all curly on the top of her head. One night, when all the other girls had gone home, Denny and I were the only ones left. We decided to walk over the stray and back to Jackie's, Denny was staying over with us. Halfway across the stray we were tired and decided to have a rest, the next thing I knew it was getting light and I could smell soil strongly. We were both propped up against a tree, we had fallen fast asleep! When we woke up and stumbled up the road to the flat, I couldn't find my keys, we had to wake Jackie up. She just opened the door and stood there laughing at us, we both had mascara all over our faces and looked like a pair of tramps. Jackie just put us both in the lounge to sleep it off and went back to bed. Fun times!

CHAPTER 11

Billy and the Good Times 1995

Donovan appeared to be moving on quicker than me. After all, he had got what he wanted, he was finally free of me and now had the kids to himself. Mission accomplished. He was dating Kit, another single parent. Donovan delighted in referring to himself as a single parent, too. Kit had four children, one of whom was profoundly deaf. The kids all started to get to know each other, as they were spending lot of time in each other's houses. Donovan didn't tell me what was going on. Tyler and Sarah had become less available at the weekends, as they were chilling with Kit and her kids. Consequently, my time with them was diminishing, just as Donovan wanted. He started telling me they were too busy or preferred to spend time with Kit and her kids, rather than be dragged around by me on a Saturday visiting family that they were drifting away from. I couldn't do much about it. He was very much in charge, I believed him when he told me that I had no rights regarding the kids. Of course, that was bollocks. That was so wrong. He had the advantage of being with the kids all the time, he could easily find ways to manipulate them and make sure that they would have more fun with him than me. His plan was working. I could see my kids drifting away from me and there seemed to be nothing I could do about it.

Tyler was still very withdrawn, very quiet. Though he had recently started playing drums with some of his friends at school, they even formed their own school band. I remember when he was only about two years old, I was in a queue in a shop and he was sitting in the pushchair, he had loads of hair that stuck up like a fan, no matter what I did to try and tame it. We were minding our own business when this punk type of dude came over to me and pointing at Tyler, he said, "Cool hair."

I laughed, agreeing with him, then as he turned to walk away, something stopped him. The stranger turned back and looking me straight in the eye, he said, "He's going to be musical and famous."

Of course, I thought he would be, he was my son, what else would he be apart from amazing!

I just smiled and said, "Thank you."

Tyler had always shown an interest in drums from a very young age, he used to bash away on my pans with a wooden spoon on the kitchen floor. Anyway, he was always tapping or pretending to drum on the desk at school, annoying the teachers so much that they got him a pair of bongos and told him to use those as they were less annoying than the constant *tap, tap, tap,* of his fingernails! Tyler didn't show much interest in anything other than drumming. He was always very distracted, or so it seemed. I tried my best to keep seeing my kids regularly, though it was becoming increasingly difficult as they were always very busy with Kit and her family. As she lived at the other end of town, it was becoming a bit of a trek backwards and forwards for them all, eventually they started to more or less live with each other, between both houses, and I never really knew where they actually were living from one day to the next!

I couldn't believe it when I found out that Donovan had moved Sarah and Tyler from their primary school to another one nearer to Kit, just to enable them to be with her kids. I didn't like the new school; I was amazed that this could have been done without my knowledge or even permission. When I asked Donovan about it, he just said to me that I gave up all my rights to the kids and any decisions about their school when I left. What planet was he on? I was so livid that I rang the new school and arranged to go in to have a look around for myself. I wanted to meet the teachers to see for myself that Sarah and Tyler were okay there. I arrived at the school and Sarah's form teacher approached me to introduce herself. She seemed nice and she was about five foot tall, a petite woman. It wasn't possible for me to see Tyler's teacher the same day, I had to arrange to do that another time. Sarah's teacher took me into a classroom, and we were standing beside a table talking about what had happened and about Sarah in general, when I suddenly became aware of a child sitting there. It was Sarah. She was looking up at me, while colouring in a book. I hadn't expected to be able to see her, I was totally shocked.

I just looked at her and said, "Oh, it's you, Sarah..."

She giggled. I gave her a massive hug and I started blubbing. Sarah didn't normally show her emotions, this time she looked as if she might as her face became slightly pink, and her eyes began to water. I hadn't expected that, as I was not prepared to see her. The teacher said she thought it was odd that I hadn't spoken to Sarah, though I honestly did not recognise her at first, I was thinking it was a naughty child that had been kept in over play time, who just happened to be sitting there. I had no idea that they had arranged for Sarah to see me. How kind. I hadn't seen Sarah in that uniform either, she looked very different to me, that's why I didn't recognise her, too. Her teacher was really lovely, apologising for not telling me to expect to see my daughter. She seemed to understand my predicament, as she promised me that she would keep me informed of any school developments, or anything she thought

I should be aware of. I was very grateful to her for that.

Shortly after that day, I met Tyler's teacher. Donovan soon after took the kids out of that school and returned them to the one near their home again. I don't know why, he wouldn't explain it to me, though I made it clear that he couldn't keep shifting schools like that, it was unsettling for the kids and unfair on them. They needed stability and to be with their friends.

Soon it became apparent that Kit and Donovan had known each other for a while, even before we split up. I was told that Donovan used to call in at Kit's house most mornings while he was delivering post, for a cup of coffee, she lived on his round. I would like to think there was nothing going on, though I am not sure. I wouldn't put it past him. Kit was really tough looking, with extremely short hair, almost like a skin head style. If I didn't know she was with Donovan, I would have thought she was a lesbian, she was not at all feminine, she didn't wear a scrap of make up, they used to look like a couple of blokes walking around together. It was a Sunday night, I was at the pub quiz with Jackie, when Kit turned up. She had been drinking for a while I think, she was staring at me from the other side of the bar. I knew she was trying to get my attention and make eye contact with me. She clearly didn't like me; I had a feeling I was going to be in trouble. I was right.

After a while of standing staring at me, Kit couldn't wait any longer and came stomping over to me, pushed me backwards against the bar and asked me what I was looking at! I just said I wasn't looking at her. Well, she went for me, shouting abuse, calling me a bad mother, saying, "What kind of mother leaves her kids, you should be ashamed of yourself, you bitch."

I couldn't believe it, though I was expecting nothing less from her, she had been completely brainwashed by Donovan, as he had told her that I had been having an affair before I left, and our breakup was all my fault. I was a bad mother and I had walked out on them, having planned my exit. That was it. I'd had enough. Finally, I was not going to stand for anymore of this crap. I pushed her back and told her to come outside if she wanted to talk to me and I would tell her exactly what happened, she owed me that much. She came outside and eventually after a load more abuse she calmed down. I told her, in no uncertain terms, the truth about why I'd left. At first, Kit told me I was a lying cow and making it all up to cover my arse. I told her I had absolutely no reason to lie, and it broke my heart completely losing the kids. I didn't care whether she believed me or not, though I was telling her the truth, I was also sick and fed up with taking the blame.

To my complete surprise, Kit actually believed me after a while, we seemed to be sitting outside that pub for ages, in fact, we must have been as it had closed, and Jackie had checked I was okay and then walked home. The next thing I knew it was about 1 am and we were still sitting there. We ended up hugging each other, Kit apologised for getting things so wrong, though she said Donovan was incredibly believable. I told her not to worry about that, I knew how manipulative he could be. We parted ways, she set off to walk home and think about what she was going to do, I went back to the flat. I felt good. Finally, I had said my piece and stuck up for myself, it felt amazing. I had finally had enough of keeping quiet.

Kit and Donovan carried on seeing each other, weirdly, though sadly after six months Kit was diagnosed with cancer. She died very quickly after her diagnosis. I was very sad for the kids, though I think Donovan and Kit had started to drift apart after our conversation and had not seen as much of each other. I knew as well that Donovan wouldn't cope very well with her being ill. He didn't do illness; he stuck his head well and truly in the sand on that front. A fact that became even more apparent later. Tyler remained to be withdrawn and quiet, I was beginning to think there was something else going on with him. Every time I asked Donovan about him, he would just say Tyler was fine and it was just the way he was. My gut feeling told me different, though I trusted that Donovan was keeping a close eye on both of the kids, and I tried not to worry about my son. Tyler had told me a few times that he was struggling when he went to the toilet and he was finding it painful also, sometimes, his urine was a very dark colour. I mentioned this to Donovan more or less every time when I dropped the kids off, he just told me everything was alright, and Tyler was making a big deal of it for attention. I asked him to get Tyler checked out with the doctor and he kept on telling me he would. He did not. Tyler was really tired all the time, I thought this wasn't quite right for a boy of his age. He should have had tons of energy, darting about on a bike with his friends.

Donovan just kept telling me to mind my own business and leave it to him. It was my bloody business, they were my kids, for fuck's sake. I was worried about Tyler; I just knew something wasn't right. I told Tyler to keep telling his dad when he wasn't feeling well and eventually, he would have to do something about it. I think Tyler just gave up after a while as he wasn't getting anywhere. Maybe he just thought that was how everyone felt. I don't know.

Amy was working at a Furniture Design Showroom in Hackness, a bespoke kitchen design company. They did other rooms, though they specialised in kitchens, they were very expensive and posh. She told me that she was leaving the job as she wanted to set up her own cleaning business and they had asked her if there was anyone, she knew who would like the job. She thought of me instantly, I had told her that I needed to leave the Solicitors, there were too many memories for me there and everyone knew too much about my situation. I didn't feel comfortable there anymore and even though they had been very supportive, I just felt like I needed a new start, a different direction. I jumped at the chance as the Showroom was a really nice environment to work in and it had a bright new showroom. I quite fancied being in reception and having more contact with people.

Remarkably, I got the job without much of an interview. The showroom was managed from the head office which was located in some swanky part of London and the area manager, Hugh, came over to interview me. He offered me the job there and then. Result! I felt liberated. A new job, new start, new chapter for me. Just what I needed. When I started my new job, Amy was there still for another two weeks to show me the ropes. It was actually bit of a doddle, there wasn't much to do apart from greet people when they came in and make them feel welcome. After that, we'd try to flog them a glamorous kitchen, or suchlike!

One day, a famous footballer came in with his wife, I couldn't believe it as she was quite normal, not the usual, glamourous type of footballer's wife, as shown in all the magazines.

They were both lovely and down to earth, they bought a very nice kitchen. I enjoyed doing the ordering and arranging deliveries, though I was a bit nervous after Amy had left, though I soon got the hang of it.

A bright red Sierra car pulled up just outside the window one morning. It was spotless, incredibly shiny and clean. I thought it may be a new client, I primed myself ready to greet them and get my sales head on. Well, this dark, incredibly handsome man emerged from the driver's seat, he was stunning! Very tall, his jet-black hair was scraped back, a bit like a young Andy Garcia. He was wearing jeans, a black T shirt, and a black and white lumber jacket over the top. Of course, he was wearing designer shades, too.

He burst through the door, threw his sunglasses on the desk and hollered out in a huge voice, "Well, hello!"

As I smiled at him, he gave me the biggest grin, I noticed his perfect teeth, and what a super confident and larger than life character he was. He flicked his hands through his hair as it flopped over his big brown eyes. He was tanned and looked like a model. Handsome didn't cover it. He was carrying a Filofax and he flung that on the desk, too. I thought to myself, this can't be a customer, this must be Billy. Everyone had told me that this larger than life, highly successful designer called Billy, would be coming over from another showroom to work in the Hackness showroom for a while. His role was to try and pick up the business. They'd all warned me that he was a bit of a handful, though I had no idea he would be like this - what a fella!

He looked straight at me and said, "We haven't met yet have we?"

I said, "No, I don't think so."

I felt really intimidated by him, I had never met anyone with such confidence and life. He was full of it. He had indeed come over from Nottingham to check out the showroom and make arrangements to start work the following week with us. How was I going to cope with him, I thought? He was so full on. Billy spent the afternoon chatting to people on the phone, with great charisma and he had already arranged several client visits by the end of the day. What a cracker. After I had got over the shock of his entrance, we started to chat and I found that we really got on well, he brought out my fun side I'd forgotten about, it had been buried for ages. We had the same sense of humour and we brought it out in each other. By the end of the day, we were mates.

Billy explained to me very early on that he was gay. Like most women would, I thought it was a waste of a good-looking guy, though it did make it easier to get to know him, I could just be myself with him. Over the next few months, Billy and I got to know each other very well, we would sing show tunes at the top of our voices when the place was quiet and spent much of our time laughing and joking together. Mostly at my expense, I didn't mind. What a top bloke, he was a real tonic, and a really nice person, too. He didn't show that much interest in my life and the kids, though he did manage to find out bits and pieces about my past. He opened up enough to tell me he was abused by his father and hated him. Billy was Scottish, his parents and most of his family were living in Scotland. Although he didn't see much of them, he adored his mother and would speak to her on the phone quite often. He didn't speak with his father. Billy had several boyfriends, nobody really special, he seemed to like to play the field and loved the challenge of a straight man. I don't think he ever turned one, it was just one of his missions in life. He had his eye on Amy's Mike. When Mike's company took the cleaning contract for the showroom, Billy would always make a play for Mike, though there was absolutely no chance there. Mike liked him, he thought Billy was funny, though he kept well away from him.

Billy was very persuasive; we began to go out for drinks after work at the bar opposite the showroom. He was living in Nottingham; he still had a flat there and spent a couple of nights a week in Hackness staying in a hotel. He charged our boozing to expenses, he got away with it somehow. Billy was wealthy, he made a lot of money and he worked hard, being very good at the job and he had such flare. He'd know instantly what people wanted. A real hit with the ladies, Billy just loved women. He was a terrible flirt, all the women thought they could turn him. I knew different. He was two hundred percent gay, he just enjoyed being around attractive people, he loved beauty in every shape and form, be it a man or a woman, he just liked looking at attractive people. He had many friends and was really popular. Billy was Mr Gay UK a few years ago, he told me that almost every day! He was very proud of this and would drop it in whenever he got a chance. Hilarious.

One of the first things he asked me to find for him was a tanning studio in Hackness as he worked out at the gym and went on the sun bed almost every day, too. I had never met anyone like Billy before, he certainly intrigued me. There were two other designers and a draughtsman called Dylan working at the Showroom at that time. Dylan was hilarious as well; he had an extremely small head and Billy used to call him pin head. He got away with it when no one else would have! Dylan would just roll his eyes and tell him to 'fuck off'.

We all used to make up plays and act them out in the showroom when it was quiet. It was such fun, we all got on really well and became great friends. We spent most nights during the week after work in the local bar. It was such a great distraction for me as I was still missing the kids, it helped me to forget for a few hours. I could just be myself again, it felt good, though I was disappearing into a bottle, and I knew it wasn't ideal. Looking back, I think I let Billy dominate me, without a doubt. He began trying to persuade me to get a flat with him, saying it'd be great for both of us, and we could share the rent. I felt bad as I was really happy with Jackie, she'd been such a good friend to me when I really needed her, it just didn't feel right to leave. Billy was very persuasive though, in the end, I just couldn't say no to him. Before I knew it, he'd arranged for us to look at a local, two bedroomed, flat. As soon as we walked in, we could see it was beautifully decorated, it was quite an old building and the flat was on the second floor. It had a huge lounge with a big leather sofa in the middle and a massive window with a dining table and four chairs. The furniture and carpets were lovely. As we went to look at the first bedroom, it was like something out of a Bond film. There was a massive king size bed with white bedding and white drapes hanging around the bed. It had a gorgeous, ensuite bathroom and I thought it would be ideal for me. The big wardrobes had plenty of storage and enough floor space to use for the kids if they wanted to come and stay over.

At the bottom of the corridor, there was a very small pokey single room, which wasn't even big enough to have wardrobes in it. It had a small ensuite with just a bath in it.

Billy took one look and said, "This'll do for you, then."

There was no discussion, he would be taking the big room and I would have the small one. I was gobsmacked, even though I expected it really as he agreed to pay the bond and two-thirds of the rent. I would pay a third, that seemed fair enough, yet I had hoped that there would be enough space in my room for the kids to stay over. Billy told me that he would be spending some of the time over in Nottingham in the flat and if I had the kids at the weekend they could come over when he wasn't there. He didn't want them in his room though, but at least they could come over. I thought that was going to be tough, I could do it, and I couldn't say no as before I turned round, he had handed the bond over and paid the first month's rent. I hadn't even told Jackie at the time, and I felt terrible, how was I going to leave her. Anyway, I went home that night and told Jackie I would be moving in with Billy, she was okay about it and more concerned that he may have a bad influence on me. She wanted me to be sure about what I was doing. She would be losing half towards her rent, as well as losing me. I was firmly under Billy's spell by then, I had no choice really after he had rushed into getting the flat. We moved in very soon after that.

What a laugh we had. Billy was such good fun and an excellent cook. We became really good friends and spent a lot of time together. He would go over to Nottingham most weekends and I would miss him while he was gone. I didn't like being on my own. He started trying to persuade me to go with him. Eventually, I agreed, and we drove over straight from work one Friday night. He loaded the car with nibbles and a bottle of champagne, put Madonna's Vogue and Bobby Brown on full volume and we drove over to his flat which he shared with another gay bloke. They were just friends though I think with the odd benefit thrown in.

When we got to the flat, we opened the champagne and went out to the first bar. It was a real eye opener; we went to the gay bars. I couldn't believe my eyes. I didn't know who was male and who was female, all of them were flamboyant with their amazing make up and massive wigs. They were a big, welcoming, happy, crowd of people, I felt surprisingly comfortable there, it was as if I had known them all for ages. Every bar we went into was friendly, there was no trouble whatsoever as the music pumped through the streets. Billy was extremely popular, he knew just about everyone, they all seemed to really like him and were over the moon to see him.

He seemed to own the street, wherever there were bouncers or a queue, Billy would just walk straight passed the queue, with me tagging behind him and we'd go directly into the bar. Billy didn't queue. Ever. I was amazed at it all, I loved everything about it, despite the pangs of guilt about feeling good and happy when I had left my kids with my ex-husband. We were just about to go to the club, when Billy said we needed to pop into another bar on the way to get some stuff. I thought he meant clothes or something, I had no clue as what he was on about. We walked into a very dark place. This bloke came straight over to Billy and gave him a small bag. Billy gave him some money and told me to go to the bar to get some lemonade. Lemonade? I thought, that's weird. He rushed over to me, told me to open my mouth. I obeyed, like a fool, as he popped something in there, then he gave me the lemonade and told me to swallow it. I thought it was a paracetamol or something to stop me getting a hangover. It was ecstasy! Within minutes, an overwhelming feeling of euphoria enveloped me. It was fantastic, I felt ten feet tall. I loved everybody. I was walking on air, everything was funny, I felt like I had known everyone for years, everything was extreme and huge.

Billy's face lit up, as he said, "You are going to have the best night you have ever had, trust me."

I felt amazing. Like a super model! We strutted along to the club, bypassed the queue. When we got inside, Billy turned to me and said, "Fuck off and have fun!"

He promptly disappeared. I didn't care, I felt invincible, I wasn't scared or worried about being on my own, I felt liberated and confident. I could do anything; I bounced onto the dance floor and danced my socks off for hours. God knows what I looked like, but I didn't give a toss. I kept catching a glimpse of Billy darting around the club and occasionally he would come over and dance with me, then shoot off again. He was manic and having an absolute ball. He kept disappearing with different blokes into the toilet. He would emerge looking flushed, his hair flopping over his face, and he'd then move on to the next bloke. He kept coming over with bottles of water, making me drink them to keep me hydrated and then he would go off again. After what seemed like hours of dancing, we finally left about 6am as the euphoric feeling would start to wear off. We were exhausted and just needed to sleep. No hangover, just incredibly tired. One night I danced so hard my big toe burst through my tights and had swollen to twice the size, I hadn't felt a thing and only saw the damage when I kicked off my shoes. Hardly surprising when I had been dancing constantly for about six hours non-stop. We would then drive back to

Hackness, have a lie down together on the king size bed, go to Asda and he would cook the most fantastic breakfast. We would spend the whole day lounging around and he would be telling me about his conquests. Later, we would go to the local gay bar. This became a regular thing, on the weekends when I didn't see the kids.

I knew I was falling off the rails, I couldn't stop myself, we were having such a ball. I couldn't believe that someone like Billy wanted to spend time with me. I was flattered, I needed to feel wanted and important to somebody, and he satisfied that feeling. We grew extremely close, I trusted him completely. I told him everything, he did the same. We would talk until the early hours; we now knew each other really well. It was like having a best girlfriend and a boyfriend all rolled into one, but without any funny business. We laughed, we cried, he would tell me I would always have a special place in his heart. He was like a brother to me. I felt the same. He used to say that if we didn't meet anyone within ten years, we would marry each other. There were moments when I thought it could have happened. I loved him and I believed he loved me, too, like a sister.

CHAPTER 12

The Demon Drink 1995

Billy and I started to burn out though we'd shone brightly together as good friends for a while. He had met a bloke called Eddie, who was lovely, such a nice lad. Quite a bit younger than Billy, it did not bother them, they fell in love. Billy stopped going to Nottingham as often, instead the two of them would go away for the weekend somewhere fancy like New York or stay at Eddie's cottage up North. They were really well suited, I was very happy for Billy, though I was sad that we weren't spending as much time with each other as we did before.

One of the last nights out we had together was a bank holiday weekend. Billy, Eddie and I went to Nottingham. Billy was very distracted with Eddie, to be honest I felt I was in the way. We did our usual thing on the Saturday night and were planning to do it all over again on the Sunday night. Bank Holidays were jumping in Nottingham it was wild. However, Billy woke me up on Saturday, to tell me that he wanted me to go back to Hackness that day and that he would buy me a bus ticket. He wanted some time on his own with Eddie in Nottingham, he thought it would be better if I wasn't there. Billy never beat around the bush, it was then that I realised I'd served my purpose, he just didn't want me around anymore. I agreed to go back to Hackness that afternoon feeling quite rejected. We had done the usual drugs the night before and, as I was feeling off colour, I really wasn't too keen on staying another night in Nottingham anyway.

On my way back home to Hackness, I started to feel quite unwell. I felt extremely dizzy, sick and I started hallucinating. I kept seeing people as reptiles with big alligator heads on them, it was very frightening. I think I must've taken a bad tablet; I was now experiencing the aftereffects as it was wearing off. I was freaking out. As I walked from the bus stop to the flat, all along the way I kept seeing snakes and reptiles on the floor and behind trees, I must have looked like I was a complete nutter as I was terrified and kept dodging them and stepping over things. I just wanted the effects of the drug to wear off. I was scared that I was going to be on my own, something awful could happen. I just wanted to get into the flat and lock myself in it until it was over. I decided I would sleep in Billy's bed; I needed the space and didn't want to be in the rather confined small room.

I slept for a couple of hours though woke up as I pulled the quilt back over me, I saw what looked like a midget version of Billy, wearing a white robe with a white towel on his head, and it was pulling the quilt off me. I was terrified, I screamed and told him to go away. I shut my eyes tightly and hoped that he would go away, he looked like a gnome and was laughing at me with a wild look on his face. It was awful. So vivid and weird. I must have fell back to sleep. I did not dare to open my eyes again, for fear of what I may see. I woke up hours later in the dark. I had got through it. I felt terrible. My heart was pounding, my head was banging but thank God, the hallucinations had stopped. I got up, made some toast and a cup of tea. I sat watching a bit of telly, I couldn't concentrate so I went back to bed. This was my wake-up call. What the hell was I doing to myself. This had to stop. I had to get a grip and take back control of my life, or God knows where it was going to end.

In the weeks that followed, Billy began working more and more out of the other showroom again, we didn't see quite as much of each other. I told him about my episode that weekend, which of course he thought was hilarious and just flippantly said I must have had a reaction to one of the tablets he had given me. Oh, and he forgot to tell me that he'd given me some speed, too. Cheers Billy.

Sheila walked into the showroom, she was a new designer, she had been appointed to cover the times when Billy wasn't there. She was really nice and reminded me of Sue Ellen Ewing from the TV show, Dallas. She wore the same smudged, black, eye make-up, she had a similar quivering mouth and manner to Sue Ellen, too. Sheila was slender and she always smelled nice, wearing the most expensive perfume. Her husband was loaded, they had a beautiful, converted barn in the countryside. We got on great, she always made me laugh. She didn't seem to be much good at the designing side of the job, however, she was very good at selling and the clients loved her. We were quiet in the showroom at that time, I was not busy, perhaps I paid more attention to my colleagues due to that. Anyway, I began to think there was something strange about Sheila. In the mornings, Sheila would arrive at work looking absolutely fabulous, spotless make-up, styled hair and wearing lovely designer clothes. After a couple of hours, she started to look like her face had dropped, as she would start to slur her words and put her head on the desk. She didn't eat lunch and by the afternoon, she'd often disappear and lay down on one of the beds in the back of the showroom for a snooze. Later, Sheila would emerge, livelier, more awake. She would then go off to collect her son, Charlie, from school. This became a regular thing.

Sheila only really worked in the mornings. In the afternoons, as I described above, she'd be asleep or off out somewhere, away from the showroom. I was constantly covering for her and when the folks from Head Office rang to ask to speak to her, I had to think on my feet and make up a site visit, or something to cover for her. Finally, the truth emerged that Sheila was an alcoholic. She used to keep a bottle of vodka in her handbag, she would top up her coffee cup throughout the day without me knowing. Finally, I discovered that she was doing this when, one day, while she was having her usual afternoon sleep, her bag fell off the bed, causing the empty bottle to fall out onto the floor! I didn't know what to do. Should I say something or not? As I didn't know her that well, I was not sure how she would take it. I made the mistake of telling Billy about it, he thought it was hilarious. I didn't say anything to Sheila, I didn't want to embarrass her.

The next time Billy came into the showroom and Sheila was there, he just blurted out, "Hello, you must be Sheila, the alky?"

I couldn't believe he did that! She was mortified, as she looked at me like I'd stabbed her in the back. After Billy left, she said she needed to drink to be able to get through the day. As we talked about it openly, it became clear that her husband was quite aggressive and manipulative with her. She said he wouldn't let her do anything she wanted to do, and she didn't really want to work at all, she wanted to be at home with her son, though her husband wouldn't let her. I felt really sorry for her, I wanted to help her. She invited me to go home with her for dinner and said I could stay the night and then come back to work with her the next day. I agreed and said we would arrange it in the next couple of weeks. Sheila promised me she wouldn't drink at work anymore. She lied.

The next day she came in, got completely hammered without my knowledge, she was pretty clever. Head Office kept ringing, asking to speak to her. No chance, she couldn't string a sentence together. I didn't know what to do so in the end I told Head Office that we had a bit of a problem, by that time she was indisposed in one of the beds in the back of the showroom. Head Office staff were fuming. I thought I was helping. She needed help. Sheila emerged from the bed, announcing that she was going to drive to go pick up Charlie from school. I refused to let her go and took her car keys away from her. She got really nasty, stomped out of the building, telling me to fuck off. I had no choice, I had to call her husband and arrange for him to pick up Charlie, otherwise he would have been waiting for his mother. I didn't know where she had gone. Her husband said he would take care of everything and thanked me for letting him know. I was so worried about her. She never came back. I felt terrible. Guilty for telling everyone.

I saw Sheila about three weeks later, when she walked past the showroom, she just waved with a beaming smile on her face as if nothing had happened. I heard through the grapevine that she had been sacked by the Showroom; her husband had agreed that she should stay at home for him to keep an eye on her. I hoped to God she was okay.

Billy and I were beginning to drift apart, he was spending more and more time with Eddie and not at the flat with me. Completely out of the blue, he turned up at work one day and asked me to go to the bar over the road with him at 1pm. I thought it would just be for a catch up though it wasn't. He called the girl behind the bar over and asked her to witness our conversation. I wondered what the hell was going on. Billy looked at me, saying that he didn't think it was working out at the flat and that he was giving me notice to leave. He said he would be moving out for six weeks and during that time I should find somewhere else to live. What the actual fuck!? Where the hell did that come from. I was absolutely stunned, not least gutted. I had received no clue that Billy wanted me out, even though I knew things had cooled off between us, I just thought that was due to his newfound love with Eddie and I was genuinely pleased for him. Now what was I supposed to do? I had no words, even if I had Billy had prepared his speech and wouldn't let me get a word in edgeways anyway.

Billy just looked at the girl behind the bar, back at me, and said, "Okay, don't bother coming back to work this afternoon, it's best if you don't."

I was speechless. Billy went on to say that he would be working from another showroom for the next six weeks. He had paid the rent up front; I didn't have to worry about that, which was good of him. I still couldn't believe it. I was so upset, no explanation, no notice. How could he be so mean. After all we had done together, how close we had become, it was really odd. I was blown away. The girl behind the bar looked at me, shrugged her shoulders and walked off. Billy left me at the bar. I wondered what on earth I was going to do.

A couple of days later, one of the contractors at the Showroom told me that he was opening another company in Hackness, which was going to be similar to the Showroom. I told him about my situation, and he said I was welcome to help him set up that company. I was dubious at first, though after about ten minutes, I thought it sounded really good! What had I got to lose, nothing? He told me that he couldn't pay me much, though he would pay me what he could, when he could, and he'd cover my rent. Fair enough I thought, I decided I'd take the job, as I no longer wanted to work at the Showroom, I knew it would be very difficult for both of us if

Billy had to come over to Hackness. The new job was going to be a risk, of course, I was used to those by now. Frankly, I didn't really care anymore, I was really down. I just needed a way out.

You never know, I thought, it could work out to be the job of my dreams, I just had to think about finding somewhere else to live. At least I would have a new job, I convinced myself it would be good, and I accepted the offer. I only had to give a week's notice, I had soon left the Showroom to start working with Ian, my new boss. The business was in the early stages, basically it consisted of an empty building with a desk, computer and telephone covered in dust. Ian convinced me that he and his partner, Fabian, were building it up slowly, and later on it was going to blow the Showroom out of the water. Happy days, I thought to myself.

Ian was the contractor and Fabian would be the designer. Fabian was Italian, flamboyant, full of charisma. His piercing blue eyes, coupled with a rather nice accent, was intriguing. However, he was short, as Ian was, too. They looked like a pair of small boys with old faces to me! Fabian was lovely to work with, though it was difficult for me to understand him. He was a nice, genuine, friendly bloke. He was a bit sweaty looking and though he smelled of garlic most of the time, I got used to it after a while. As we had plenty of time to talk in the early days of opening the office, I came to know Fabian quite well. At that time, he was going through a divorce, his soon to be ex-wife and his three children lived in Italy. Fabian had in a flat in Hackness, he was dating Nat, who lived locally, too. She frequently called into the showroom, I can't remember what she did for a living, though she appeared to have oodles of spare time. I liked her, she was lovely, we became good friends. We would all go out to the pub together with Ian and his wife Paula. Just for a couple of drinks to relax at the end of the day. Fabian never drank alcohol on our visits to the pub, he'd always have a glass of cold water and fidget around. I thought he was hyperactive. He kept telling me that he was teetotal and didn't drink at all. I didn't think much of it and thought good for him actually.

Things were starting to develop at the showroom, we began to fill it with displays, it was coming together well. We were planning the opening day for about a month after I started working there. It was going to be a big launch; we were working on lots of advertising and liaising with the local radio station to promote the company on there. It was really fun. Ian's eldest son was a very smart lad, he'd often come in to help me with the orders for the fittings and any other things that needed doing. I thought he would end up taking over from his dad one day, as he showed great talent, he was interested in the whole business, too. He used to say it would be his company eventually, he was enthusiastically invested in it.

When my birthday came around, August bank holiday time, Fabian asked if I was going out to celebrate. I told him I wasn't doing anything. In fact, I was spending my spare time looking for somewhere else to live for a start, I was also short of money, living on my credit card. I was missing my kids and I didn't feel like doing much at all, especially celebrating another birthday. Fabian thought it was a shame and that I should be celebrating. He persuaded me to go to the pub with him after work just for one drink. Fabian had told me before that night that the reason he only drank water was due to the fact that he was an alcoholic and it was dangerous for him to drink. That's why, on my birthday, I assumed he'd be sticking to water. No problem. How wrong could I be. We got to the bar and sat down. Fabian told me that he felt like having a drink, as it was my birthday. I asked him if that was wise after what he had told me.

Fabian replied, "Of course it's fine, I know exactly what I'm doing, it's not a problem, it's your birthday, let's celebrate it! I'll order a bottle of wine. I'm in control"

Oh, sweet lord. I was concerned, though I had no idea what was about to transpire. He drank his first glass of wine as if it was a glass of water, straight down in one, he poured another one straight away. I had only had a sip of mine. This happened again. Before I knew it, Fabian had drunk the whole bottle and had ordered another one. Oh Jesus, how was I going to get out of this one? I went to the toilet to have a think about what to do. I did a lot of my thinking on the loo! I wondered if I should just leave him to it, go out the door without him knowing, or stay and try to look after him? I didn't know what to do.

I went back to see if he was ok. I couldn't leave him. Fabian was on the phone to Nat, and he was getting animated. He was telling her it was okay and to stop bothering him. He had told her where we were and within minutes she turned up. She was livid. She stormed over to us and asked me why the hell I had given him a drink. I told her I didn't, he had ordered the wine himself, I told Nat it wasn't my fault. Fabian went to the toilet. Nat told me that we needed to stop him drinking pronto, otherwise we were both in trouble as he would get out of control. I thought she was overreacting; I was to learn later that night that she definitely was not. Fabian became aggressive, refusing to leave the pub until we ordered another bottle, insisting that we drink it with him. People were looking over at us. Nat advised me that we should do it, otherwise he could turn really nasty. She told me to trust her, she knew what she was doing.

Fabian was becoming inebriated, one minute he was nice, the next he was behaving in a vile manner towards Nat. When I tried to leave the pub, Fabian shouted at me, telling me to sit down and stay with them, repeating that as we were out celebrating my birthday, I could not leave. I was beginning to feel scared of him, I just did as I was told.

By closing time, Fabian was in a right state. As Nat and I watching him falling all over the place, he started to act abusive and aggressive to us both and the bar staff. We decided the best thing was to take him home to let sleep it off. We managed to get him into the front seat of a taxi, we climbed into the back. The car was going past an off licence, when Fabian told the driver to stop, he needed to get out. We told the driver to keep going, Fabian kept insisting that he was 'the boss' and wanted to get out. The driver just said he had no choice and stopped the cab. Fabian got out, bolted straight into the off licence, as we froze in the back as we waited for him. After a few minutes, Fabian returned carrying a bag of three bottles of whiskey and two bottles of wine. Surely, he wasn't going to drink all that alcohol. It wouldn't be possible!

The taxi arrived at Fabian's flat, Nat paid the driver and we helped Fabian up the stairs. He insisted we both came in with him for a cup of coffee. We went into the lounge to sit down.

Of course, Fabian opened one of the bottles of whiskey, barking at us to get the wine open, we were going to party. Oh God, I thought, we are in trouble now. When Fabian went into the bathroom, I looked at Nat.

"I don't want any wine," I said, "I've got to go home, I have work in the morning!"

I stood up, ready to leave.

"No, Sophia, stay – just go with it, he'll fall asleep in a while."

I didn't know what to do.

Nat looked up and me and snapped, "Besides, you got me into this mess, you have got to stay now to help me with him!"

Guilt ridden I sat down and thought, what a nightmare of a birthday! Fabian came back in, he began to drink the whiskey, the more he drank, the more unreasonable he got. He started demanding that we phone the pope and tell him ridiculous things. He was insane with drink. Jabbering on in Italian and ordering us around. I'd never seen anything like it, I was now really worried that we were actually in serious trouble. Fabian didn't know what he was saying or doing. He had lost his mind. I told him I was going to the toilet, instead I tried to leave the flat. He'd locked the front door to stop us leaving! Shit. We were definitely in trouble now. What the hell? Eventually, after much negotiation, humouring him and pretending to be on the phone to the bloody Pope, Fabian fell asleep. We searched for the front door key; we couldn't find it! He'd hidden it! Nat was shattered, she just fell asleep on the sofa. There was clearly nothing more I could do, I went into the spare room, deciding it would be best to try and get some sleep, convincing myself that everything would be better in the morning. Fabian would sober up and feel a right idiot, we could all go back to normal. Not a hope in hell. When I woke up, Fabian had been awake a while and he had started drinking again.

"I have to go home, Fabian, I have to go and open the showroom up," I told him.

He ordered me, "Sit down and shut the fuck up, you don't have to go anywhere, I'm your boss so it's up to me to tell you when you can go to work."

Next minute he was in the kitchen cutting up red onions and eating them raw. Unbelievable. Bearing in mind that Fabian had a carving knife in his hand, I thought the best thing to do was to sit down. I seemed to have been sitting there for hours, Nat was awake by then, too. She was sitting on the sofa; I was in the armchair. We both kept trying to reason with him though it was impossible as he wouldn't listen to anything we had to say. Without a doubt, he was completely bonkers. I was starting to be seriously concerned. I kept thinking about my kids, I knew I had to get out of this situation. I wasn't going to let this lunatic hurt me, not a chance. By the afternoon Fabian was wading his way through all the bottles of booze and the hours passed us all by. He was talking complete nonsense, making stupid statements and demands. I thought it was never going to end. I was mentally exhausted, as was Nat. It was like babysitting a huge, naughty child. Nat kept reassuring me that he was an okay bloke really, he wouldn't hurt us, we just needed to get him to sober up somehow and we would be fine. Yeah, right. That didn't seem possible, though I hoped she was right.

As we were both hungry, Nat suggested we go into the kitchen to try and get some food inside him. He refused to drink the coffee we made for us all. The kitchen cupboards were bare apart from some soup that we warmed up. In those days, there we no mobile phones, I couldn't call Ian or anyone else, to let them know I couldn't come into work. The day just slipped away, the next thing we knew it was dark. Nat was trying her best to get Fabian to let us out of the flat, he just kept on refusing, telling her to 'fuck off and sit down'. We didn't want to upset him.

Another night passed and Fabian had run out of booze. He told Nat to go and get him some more, she asked him for the keys for her to go to the off licence, to my surprise he gave them to her. Of course, he did, he needed more booze. She told me that she would be back, though I needed to stay with him. Though it didn't seem like a good idea to me at all, I had no choice except to agree. I wanted to help him. Fabian locked the door behind Nat with his spare key, which he seemed to produce from nowhere. I was now locked in with him.

A couple of hours passed, and Nat had not returned yet. Fabian told me that when he was living in Italy and he got drunk, he would just rock up at the hospital, they would give him a blood transfusion to replace his blood. It stopped him from going through the hangover stage. I found that hard to believe, though, have to say that he was very convincing. He threw his car keys at me, telling me to drive him to the hospital for the same treatment he'd had in Italy. I knew that it was a long shot, we hadn't a hope in hell of them doing that here. Fabian insisted they would and told me I had to help him as he couldn't face the road, he had to take to become sober again.

Fabian moved into the emotional stage, saying that he couldn't cope unless they replaced his blood. I thought if I took him to the hospital, they may keep him in, I could just leave him there and get the hell away from him. I agreed, we went downstairs to get the car and I drove Fabian to the hospital. When we walked into the Accidents & Emergency department, it was clear to everyone around us that Fabian had been drinking, as he stank of alcohol and onions! It was no surprise to me, that he was refused treatment until he'd sobered up. He was kicking off, telling them that he needed a transfusion, and he would pay for it. I was mortified. They just told me to take him back home and get him to sober up. There was nothing they could do for him. I felt stupid taking him there in the first place, though I had hoped my plan would work, it was a way out of this bloody fiasco. I didn't know what to do, I just put him back in the car to drive him back home. He was angry, crying and in a right state. Nat was back in the flat when we returned, I told her where we had been and she said she would look after him, finally agreeing that I had done enough, she told me to go home. Thank holy God for that. I was so glad to be out of that situation. I was totally exhausted, as I had been holed up in Fabian's flat for two days. I went home, had a shower and cleaned myself up and went in to work.

When Ian saw me, he just said, "Thank God, you're okay, where have you been?"

After I'd told him what had happened, he was absolutely gobsmacked. He knew that Fabian had a drink problem, though he had no idea how bad it actually was, none of us did. He told me that I had a lucky escape and to take the rest of the day off, go home for some sleep, he would see me tomorrow. What a huge relief, I went home to rest. Next morning, when my alarm woke me up, I had that awful feeling of dread again, the same one I had on the day of Donovan's accident. I felt uneasy, anxious and nervous, as if something bad was about to happen. It was about 7.30 am, when I put on the local radio station while getting ready to go to work. The local news report came on, I heard them say there had been an accident in the early hours and someone had died. Ian lived on the main street where the accident happened with his wife and the boys. I was seriously worried. I had Ian's home phone number, I called him to see if he had heard anything from Fabian. It seemed to take ages for someone to answer. Ian answered. I knew as soon as I heard his voice that something terrible had happened. He could hardly speak. He was in total shock. Apparently, Fabian had continued to drink for the rest of the day after I had left him with Nat. She had given up on him sobering up and she had left the flat shortly after me, as she knew she couldn't do anything to help him. He was totally out of it. He had trashed his flat, unplugging all the light fittings, removing all the light bulbs, apparently, he had then left the flat himself and walked about four miles away.

Fabian turned up at Ian's house and was banging on the door about 5 am that morning. It was just getting light, Ian told me, when he woke up to hear Fabian shouting, causing a right commotion outside the house. Ian's wife and the boys had all woken up and gone to the bedroom windows to see what was going on. That's just what Fabian had wanted them to do. He needed all of them to be at the window. He wanted an audience. He was shouting abuse and knocking on the door, Ian shouted out of one of the bedroom windows for him to keep quiet and go away and told Fabian that he wouldn't open the door until he had calmed down.

Fabian was nuts and a loose cannon. Ian didn't know what he was going to do. He decided to call the police and just as he picked up the phone to do that, Fabian stood still for a minute, looked up at the window and put both his arms out to the sides, like Jesus on the cross. He went quiet, just staring up at the windows. Then, he turned away, slowly walking into the middle of the road, where he lay down on his back. Ian shouted out of the window for Fabian to get up off the road. Ian panicked completely, he could see headlights coming towards Fabian, he ran downstairs and opened the front door. Before Ian could get to him, a car came from nowhere and ran straight over Fabian, dragging his body down the road until the car stopped a few houses down.

It was a 17-year-old girl who was driving the car. She had only just passed her test. The impact had killed Fabian. The girl was screaming at the wheel, she thought she had run over a bin liner in the road. Ian fell to the ground unable to believe what he had seen. His wife and boys were silent standing at the bedroom windows. Fabian was buried incredibly quickly due to his religious beliefs. As no women were allowed at the funeral either, his wife and family were not able to come over from Italy to attend. Apparently, when his wife was informed about Fabian's untimely death, she wasn't surprised, showing hardly any feelings about it. God only knows what sort of a life she had experienced with him. After what I'd seen in those two days, I can only imagine it must have been a living nightmare for her. Their poor children must have seen some stuff, too. Everyone here was in utter shock - what the hell had just happened? I couldn't believe it. How could somebody do such a thing?

Totally shocked, Ian was in bits, as was his family. He felt furious that Fabian had staged it, right outside his house. He was incensed that Fabian had made dammed sure that all Ian's family were watching him when he did it. *How hideous.* Ian's grief came out in anger at first - *how were his boys going to forget that image?* It was something that would live with them all for a long time. Without a doubt that poor girl driving the car would be a mess for a while afterwards, too.

We did not open the showroom for a few days, we all needed some time to process what had happened. Ian had lost his business partner, it turned out that Fabian was up to his eyeballs in debt and had made a few enemies along his alcohol fuelled path. Ian had not known about any of this. We concluded that it was likely that all these things were the main reasons Fabian had flipped out and decided to take his own life. We will never know. I wondered what the hell I was going to do as I wasn't sure if Ian was going to carry on with the business after Fabian's death. I felt guilty and as if it was all my fault, as if I had not gone out to celebrate my birthday with Fabian, maybe this wouldn't have happened. Ian and everyone else kept telling me not to blame myself, if it hadn't been my birthday Fabian surely would have found another excuse to have a drink. He'd planned it. Given the mess Fabian was in financially, plus he was on the brink of a divorce, it was an accident waiting to happen. I still felt terrible around Ian, *how could we all move on from this like nothing had just happened*? That's why I decided to start looking for work elsewhere. As I needed money, I took a temporary secretarial job with a local solicitor through an agency. It was really boring, just audio work, though it was a job, and the pay was okay. The people were nice enough. I was lucky as I got paid weekly, after the first week of working there, the cash started to roll back into my bank account. I still needed to find somewhere new to live though.

Though I hadn't seen much of Jackie, or her sister Amy, ever since I'd moved into Billy's flat, I considered going back to her place. However, I just didn't feel right about asking her as I didn't want her to think I was using her. I really would have loved to go back to Jackie's place, as I needed a friend right now. Since I'd met Billy, we'd become such close best mates, that I'd drifted away from most of my friends. I know now it was a stupid thing to have done, I just didn't think it would end like it did with him. When I reflected on our connection, I realised I really didn't think at all in that relationship. I was swept away with his whacky personality and all the attention he gave me; we built an amazing friendship together that put all my other friend connections into the shade. Billy had made me feel really wanted and deeply loved all I had ever needed.

Things with the kids were just as difficult. Donovan had met another woman, Julia, who worked in the bakery department at a local supermarket. Julia had three daughters and was recently divorced. I didn't know her at all though, apparently, she knew me. Donovan, as usual, went hell for leather into the relationship. Within weeks after they'd met, Julia and the girls were staying at his house frequently. Tyler hated being the only boy amongst Julia's three girls and Sarah. The girls would gang up on him and bully him. Later, I discovered that

Julia would drive all the girls to school in the car and make Tyler walk there telling him there wasn't room for him. I wish I had known that at the time, I would have kicked off big time. How cruel. Julia did other things for the girls, leaving Tyler out, such as when she made the girls their lunches, he'd get nothing. Of course, no one told me about it at the time, yet it kills me to think he was being excluded like this. My boy was really down and lonely and I didn't know. When I asked him, Donovan just kept on trying to convince me that Tyler was okay, he was just being a moody kid. Tyler wasn't feeling great, he was always very lethargic and tired. He had no enthusiasm for going out with his friends or anything. He seemed very withdrawn. I was worried about him. The only thing he was enthusiastic about was his drumming, he was good at it by all accounts.

Tyler was a very quiet boy. He kept telling me that he didn't feel well that he was always tired and felt rough. He couldn't really pin down what was wrong with him. It was difficult to understand how he felt. Every time I took Tyler and Sarah back home to Donovan, I asked him about Tyler's health. All Donovan would say was that his son was fine, he was living in a house full of girls and he was attention seeking, there was nothing wrong with him and he would be fine. I had no choice but to trust Donovan on this matter and believe that he was right. I did make him promise that he'd let me know if anything changed, as he would keep an eye on Tyler now. Donovan told me that he would. In my heart I knew he wouldn't, as I thought to myself at the time, 'Bollocks, he has no intention of keeping an eye on Tyler or letting me know.'

I carried on seeing them as much as I could, as it was hit and miss as to whether I would see them as not. Donovan was in control, and he kept on telling me that Tyler and Sarah didn't want to see me, he'd call me always on the last minute. Disappointing and disturbing for them and for me. I didn't want to believe that my own children did not want to see me. I had no choice, I had to just accept it, hoping that I would see them the week after. Nine times out of ten I didn't due to Donovan always having made other arrangements. Sometimes, he would tell me they were too tired and referred to be at home with him. That hurt. I was witnessing as they disappeared from my life.

Meanwhile, I had to try to sort myself out, I needed to get a good job and a new home. If I had a house, I could have them to stay whenever they wanted to come. That was my plan. I needed to see more of them. It was still niggling me that something wasn't right with Tyler, I just knew it. I guess it could have been Mother's intuition. I was banging my head against a brick wall trying to get information out of Donovan. I wanted him to take Tyler to the doctor immediately to get him checked out.

Most days, I looked through the job vacancies column in the local paper, there never seemed to be anything suitable for me. As I needed to find somewhere to live, too, I thought I'd look for a job with a flat attached, or something along those lines.

PART THREE – THE LUCKY ONE

CHAPTER 13

Sean Connery and A New Romance 1996

O ne day, I saw an advert for a PA, working for a local businessman, it was a live-in position. Boom! Ideal. I rang the number on the advert. A softly spoken voice answered. I explained I was calling about the job advertised, he seemed really nice and chatty, we got on very well on the telephone. He asked me general questions, then told me that he had three businesses, one of which was a night club. He needed somebody who could help him with all three businesses, doing admin and generally looking after him and the businesses. I asked him about the living conditions. He said that the right person would have a room in his large house, it would be a *hands-on* role, he would need someone he could trust. I didn't think too much about the living conditions, I just told him my personal situation and that I would need enough space to have my kids come to visit me. He replied that wouldn't be a problem at all, he liked kids, even though he didn't have any of his own. Result, I thought to myself. This will do nicely.

We spoke for ages on the phone, he seemed fine, the job would be interesting. I didn't have any doubt that I could do it. It sounded quite exciting and right up my boulevard. I was excited about it. He asked me to go along to the Club the following night to meet him to chat about the job and everything.

Just before he put the phone down, he said, "Oh by the way, some people have told me I look at bit like Sean Connery."

I thought that was a bit odd, it wasn't really relevant, though I didn't think too much about it. I just thought that would be a bonus, nothing more. After all, this was a business arrangement. As I only had a tenner in my purse until my payday the following week, I wondered how the hell I was going to get there for the interview the following night. I had to be there at 7:30 pm, before the club got busy. He said he would meet me there to discuss the job and terms. It sounded like a done deal. I just knew I had to find a way to get there, it was important that I didn't let this opportunity slip. It could sort all my problems out. At last, I'd have somewhere to live, somewhere to take the kids, plus a decent job and salary. I knew a local taxi driver from my days when I worked at the taxi office and he'd always said to me that he would take me anywhere I wanted and if I was stuck, and that all I had to do was to throw him a tenner to cover petrol. Well, as that was all I had, I thought it would be okay. I rang the taxi driver to ask him if he could take me to the interview the following night. I said I needed to be there for an interview at 7:30 pm and could he pick me up at about 7 pm. I asked him if he would come back for me after the interview to take me home, too. He agreed to my arrangements, and he confirmed it would only cost me a tenner. Done! Happy days.

I was really looking forward to the interview, as I had a really good feeling about the whole thing. I hoped that it would be just what I needed to get me on my feet and some normality into my life after everything that happened with Billy, then the tragedy of Fabian's death, I needed something good to happen for me and the kids. I arrived at the club at 7:25 pm, not too early. As the doors were locked, I was waiting outside. I caught sight of a man in the bar area, he was wearing a light purple velvet jacket and white shirt, with black 'slacks'. He had his back to me, though I remember thinking he looked quite posh from the back with his salt and pepper hair, which was very short and looked like it was thinning on the top. This must be the bloke that looked like Sean Connery! Well, when he turned round and came to the door, he looked more like Jim Bowen! I giggled to myself when I saw him, he was nothing like Sean Connery. Alarm bells rang as he burst out of the doors and greeted me with an extremely weak handshake.

Actually, it was a bit creepy as he looked me up and down as if I was a new filly!

Jesus Christ, what had I done, this suddenly didn't seem like a good idea anymore! The taxi had driven away after I'd arranged to call him when I was ready for him to pick me up. That was about now as far as I was concerned. Too late. Oh, shit what have I got myself in to now?

"Hello, you must be Sophia, I'm Adrian," he said, smiling. "Come into the office."

I thought I may as well see what the job was about while I was there, after all I may be wrong, though I just knew that I had made a mistake. As I walked through the doors there were two or three bouncers milling around, they were getting ready for the club to open. One of them came towards me as if he knew me, as I walked past him to go into the office with Adrian.

With a beaming smile on his face, he said, "Hello."

Adrian and I sat down, and he started the interview. It very soon became very clear to me that this was not going to be a normal interview. He began asking me personal questions, he took hold of my hand.

"Hmm.. you'll need to get your nails sorted out, I like long nails," Adrian advised.

That was it, I knew this was more than just a bloody job, he wanted more than that. Somehow, I got through the rest of the interview without throwing up at his slimy remarks.

Adrian, smiling, said, "Well, Sophia, I want you to take this job. Why don't you go back into the bar for drinks on the house, stay as long as you like?"

I was absolutely gutted; I had been duped. This was a huge mistake. I went through to the bar and ordered a large white wine; I may as well stay for a bit if the drinks were free. Why not, I had nothing to lose once again, free drinks and a lift home later, though I had still not got a damn job and had the problem of finding somewhere to live. I became aware of someone watching me from the other side of the bar. *Oh God*, I thought, that's all I need, some bloke trying to chat me up. I decided to leave. I was just going to the pay phone to call the taxi to take me home when this guy jumped in front of me. It was the bouncer I had seen earlier, the one who'd said hello to me as if he knew me. I certainly didn't know him; I didn't know any bouncers at all. In fact, I didn't like them, I always thought they were arrogant.

"Hello," he said again, "I'm Paul."

"Hello, do I know you?"

"Not yet, but you will by the end of the night," he grinned, cheekily.

I laughed, thinking he's a cocky piece of work. As we chatted, I was studying him. Paul was the polar opposite of my type. He was very tall, with gingery blonde hair, his nose was huge, and he had very misshaped teeth.

No oil painting, I thought to myself, though he appeared to be a genuine and nice bloke.

"So, Sophia, what are you doing here?" he asked.

"Well, I came to see Adrian for an interview for the PA job," I replied.

He laughed, saying, "Another one!"

I tried to laugh, though I didn't think it was funny just very strange.

Paul continued, "Adrian is well known for trying to find a woman for himself, under the guise of a professional interview and job offer, all he really wants is a woman to live with him."

I wasn't shocked, just annoyed, I said, "Hmm... well, that explains it! I gathered something like this from the way he was doing the interview. I'm going to ring mtaxi and get the hell out of here. What a creep! Ugh... "

"Yes, he is... But look, you're here now, why don't you stay and have a few more drinks? I'll keep an eye on you and I like talking to you," Paul suggested.

"Oh, I don't know, you can't talk if you're working, can you? I'll just be sitting here alone."

"You don't have anything to lose though if you stay, do you? You may as well have the free drinks, something at least from this dire situation. It's usually a good night tonight at the club..." he coaxed.

He had a persuasive way with him. I decided to stay for a couple more. I felt like I had absolutely nothing to lose, it wouldn't do any harm to stay for a bit longer. It was a fun place and started to fill up until it was packed. Paul guarded me for most of the night, nipping over to talk to me now and again. He had a break and came over for a drink. He told me that he was in a relationship though he wasn't happy. He was ex forces in the RAF Regiment. He seemed like a very hard person; he wouldn't take any shit. It suited him being a bouncer. He said he worked as a lorry driver during the day, he was a bouncer for something to do in the evenings and for the extra cash. He was a body builder, he had great big shoulders, though I don't think he worked hard enough on his legs, they were very skinny, he looked top heavy, almost cartoon like! I liked him though, he made me laugh. I felt weirdly safe around him, he was kind, and I could tell he had a good heart. It was getting late, and we were getting closer.

Paul said, "It was a beautiful sunset tonight when I was driving to work, I had funny feeling that I was going to meet someone special who will change my life."

I nearly rolled my eyes, as I thought, What a load of codswallop! I just went along with it. He was a bit of a dreamer, nice bloke, though. At the end of the night, Adrian had been mooching around, chatting up women. He kept coming past me and touching my bum, he gave me the creeps completely and I had made my mind up that I wouldn't be pursuing my career with him. Not a chance. I think he had got the message by the end of the night, as I was very cold with him and made it quite clear that I was not for sale, I wouldn't be taking the job as his 'PA'. I could tell he was irritated by me talking to Paul, thank God, he backed off.

I had rung my taxi man; everyone was beginning to leave the club. I was waiting in the doorway for my taxi to arrive when Paul came bounding over to me to ask for my number. I didn't really want to give it to him it, I also didn't want the hassle of him trying to persuade me to give it to him either. The easiest thing to do would be to just give him the number as I thought he would have second thoughts and not call me. After all, he had told me that he was living with a woman at the time, there was no way I wanted that sort of complication, and I wouldn't get involved with somebody who was already in a relationship anyway. That's not cool. I got into the taxi, as I waved at him as the car drove off, Paul looked like an excited puppy. I had a funny feeling of my own, then, as I felt that I would actually be seeing him again. When I got back the flat, I felt quite deflated. All my hopes for a new life and job were gone, I had made another mistake. Never mind, I could see the funny side of it, I was chuckling to myself about Adrian's velvet Austin Powers style jacket and his description of himself. How funny and deluded was he. I chuckled myself to sleep, looking forward to a lie in as it was Sunday the next day and, unfortunately, I wasn't able to see the kids. I would still have a nice, quiet day at home and have another think about what I should do next to improve my situation. It must have been about 11 am when I heard the phone ring. I picked it up, I knew it was a call from a phone box as I heard somebody trying to put the money in the slot and I heard the pips going. I thought it was a crank call, I just put the phone down. It rang again a minute later. This time the call connected; it was Paul!

He said, "Hello, I told you that you would be with me by the end of the night last night and you will be."

I thought he was very full of himself and sure about it.

"Hello, Paul. It was nice to meet you, but I'm not interested, you are already in a relationship. My life is really too complicated already, you're better off out of it!" I told him, hoping it would be enough to put him off.

"Oh, don't worry about that, I will sort it all out. Can I come round to see you?" he insisted, he was not going to give up!

"I'm really busy, Paul. Maybe we can meet up when you have sorted yourself out?" I responded.

"Look out your window, I'm just down the road in my car. Look, it's a red soft top!"

I went to the window and looked down the road, there was Paul in the phone box, and I could see his car. How the hell had he found me? Apparently, he had followed my taxi last night, that's how he knew where I lived. That was a bit weird and almost worrying! It explained so much about his character. On the other hand, I was flattered I guess, I thought he must be keen, why not give him a chance, he could be a good friend, if nothing else, and I certainly needed one of those. I didn't fancy him at all.

"Okay, give me half an hour or so, and you can call round for a cup of tea," I said.

He was happy and agreed. I put some of my lippy on, tidied the flat up and got out some cups and started to make the tea. Bang on thirty minutes later, Paul was at the door. Looking different in his non bouncer clothes, he was now wearing a leather jacket T shirt and jeans. I was correct, he obviously didn't work on his legs when he trained, as he looked very top heavy with skinny legs. Quite odd. We drank our tea and ended up chatting for hours, he was really easy to talk to and had plenty to say for himself. As I didn't fancy him at all, I felt completely at ease with him, I could tell him anything about me and my life. I almost tried to put him off me by being brutally honest about my situation, telling him that he would be better off not getting involved with me. He wouldn't be put off by anything I said. As I spoke about my split with Donovan, the kid's situation and Billy, I even talked about Fabian, I noticed Paul just took all of it in his stride.

He kept repeating that, "Shit happens."

I began to wonder if he was actually really listening to me. I thought he was either very understanding or completely weird and didn't give a toss about my past, not sure which at that point. He was living with a woman at that time, though he told me it was going nowhere, she drank too much for his liking and he wasn't happy with her at all. She sounded classy, she smoked, drank lager from the can and left cans all over the place. Horrific. Paul clarified that he wanted out of the situation, indeed, soon he would be moving on. He owned a studio apartment in Tankarsley with a tenant who would be leaving at the end of the month and Paul would move in there. As far as he was concerned, it was all over with his current girlfriend, though he hadn't told her yet. Meeting me had made his mind up, he would tell her today. Woah! Hold on, I thought to myself, this is all a bit sudden. I liked Paul though I wasn't sure about getting involved with him. There was something not quite right about him, he seemed too good to be true. He told me all about his life, telling me that he was unloved, his mother was an alcoholic and died years ago. His father, Angus, was too old when Paul was born, and he'd never loved him. Paul said his father had made it perfectly clear that he never wanted Paul.

One of Paul's first memories was being left in the house on his own, he was only five years old. His Mum and Dad had gone out to the pub, he was scared and remembered sitting on the stairs, crying, in the dark and wondering where they were. Paul was scared of his father who had been in the Horse Guards and had a very military manner. Angus was a successful businessman; he had built an engineering business from nothing. He enjoyed the finer things in life, but not children, or especially his son. He loved classic cars and had an Armstrong Siddleley Sapphire car, which he hardly ever took out of the garage. Paul told me it was a beauty, the bodywork was a pale green colour, with a cream leather interior and a mahogany dash. Angus attended the odd car show with it, swanning around like JR Ewing, wearing a great big white cowboy hat. Not the best-looking bloke, he just thought he was! Bit of a ladies' man, too. Growing up Paul never spent any time with his dad, he felt very unloved and unwanted. He remembered his dad used to hit his mother; she was always drunk. I felt sorry for him.

He told me that he thinks he suffered brain damage when his mother was pregnant, due to all the alcohol she drank during the pregnancy. Bit of a weird thing to say. Angus now lived in Somerset with his dog Winnie. Paul hated that dog; I think he was jealous of it as his dad thought the world of it. He had a stepbrother called Ronald, who was extremely wealthy and had his own engineering business. Paul didn't see much of him; they didn't really get along. Paul said they saw each other occasionally; it was strained between them. Ronald was also into classic cars and had a fleet of them in a great big, carpeted garage, it was the size of an aeroplane hangar on his estate. It was like something off the telly programme Top Gear. Ronald used to take the cars out now and again, I think he may have done the odd wedding with them, just for the prestige, certainly not for the money. Apparently, over the years, there had been many family disagreements. From what I could gather, Paul was in the middle of all of them.

Paul discovered that Ronald was having an affair with his secretary and took it upon himself to tell Ampika, Ronald's wife. It caused no end of chaos. Understandably, they didn't want much to do with Paul after that, even though he swears blind it was true and Ronald was denying it. There was a stepsister, too, who lived in the South and he didn't see much of her either. They appeared to be a complicated family. Paul came across as being a bit of a lost soul. His childhood was made up of mostly bad memories, he didn't have many friends, struggled all the way through school with behavioural issues, resulting in terrible school reports. Paul's father constantly called him thick and a waste of space. Despite having extremely low self-confidence, Paul had an arrogance about him, almost like he had a chip on his shoulder, a belief that everyone owed him something. I read that as self-preservation. After a while, I got the impression that Paul just wanted to be loved and I started to really warm to him, I wanted to make him feel better and help him.

One day, his friend decided to join the RAF and seventeen-year-old Paul tagged along when his friend went to sign up. Paul had left school and was at a loss as to what to do himself, he was miserable at home so he went along to see whether it would be something of interest to him. Before he arrived, he had no intention of signing up, though when he heard about all the career opportunities in the RAF, he thought it seemed like a good idea. It was a chance for him to leave home, see a bit of the world and get away from his abusive father. Result. Paul signed up to become a Gunner, he was interested in guns. Military life would suit him, being as tough, mentally and physically, as he was, after the way he'd been brought up. Even so, Paul said that the initial training was brutal. Six weeks of hell. Living in holes in the ground, the trainees had to dig their own beds in trenches, kill wildlife and eat it. The aim was to break them. Many people crumbled and left. Not Paul, he was hard as nails, he took blow after blow, just wouldn't give up. The more people that left, the more he was determined to stay. Paul was thoroughly brainwashed. He got through the initial training with flying colours and became a 2 Para, they called them rock apes, they were like the SAS. They were machines, they had all the emotion knocked out of them during the training course. He seemed proud of that, he liked it. I realised that he became detached from any emotion he had, it didn't sound much to be proud of to me.

After the training Paul was posted all over the place. He seemed to have been hit with the lucky stick. In 1979, he had been due to be travelling on the ferry from Zeebrugge to Kent. At the last minute the plan was changed, they sent him to Northern Ireland instead. Paul's friend took his place on the ferry and perished. That could have been Paul. He did five tours of Northern Ireland during the Troubles; he saw some terrible things. After Paul had a few lucky escapes, he thought that he had been blessed by an angel. Somebody had been looking out for him. Maybe it was his mother watching over him? Who knows?

While he was abroad, Paul met a woman, and they were seeing each other. One weekend, his girlfriend flew over to see him. They decided to go out with a group of friends to a local bar, their cars were all parked side by side in the car park. While the majority of the group wanted to head off to a local club, Paul and his girlfriend decided they would get a takeaway instead and go back to her place instead, they would leave about thirty minutes before the rest of them. They said their goodbyes to everyone, then they went off to buy their takeaway. The next morning Paul went into the NAFFI for breakfast. Everyone looked stunned to see him. He asked why they all were looking at him like that. It turned out that after Paul and his girlfriend had left the pub and driven away, the others had all got into their cars and minutes later were blown to high heaven, the IRA had planted bombs under all the cars apart from Paul's, they all got blown up and died. He was devastated. He had lost most of his friends and their girlfriends. Why was he the lucky one? Why didn't he die? Paul felt guilty for years after. He never got over that.

During another tour, Paul was involved in gun fire and saw his friend's helmet on the ground near to him. He picked it up, only to discover that his friend's head was still in it. Horrifying. He never got counselling or any help for either of these hideous events. He should have, without a doubt. As I was to find out later. Paul was damaged goods.

CHAPTER 14

Black Magic Chocolates 1996

Paul and I started to see each other regularly, I couldn't get rid of him. Keen wasn't the word; it was *borderline desperate.* It put me off a bit, to be honest, though I enjoyed the company, and I didn't have the heart to tell him not to come over. I felt sorry for Paul. He must have come over every night for the following week after that first Sunday when he'd told me his life story. That week Paul was on an early shift, after work he'd go to the gym to pump up his shoulders and arms, not his legs! After the gym, he'd come and pick me up from my job. On the way back to my place, we went to the supermarket to buy food for dinner, which I'd cook for us. We would spend most of the evening talking.

As money was a bit short for him at that time, I would buy the food, it felt good to be looking after someone again. Paul was very easy to talk to, I just felt very comfortable and safe with him. He did fuck up at times though. One day, he turned up at my workplace, all dressed in black and holding a red rose, I think he thought he was the man in the *Black Magic* chocolates advert. I was mortified. It was way too cheesy and far too early for that kind of thing!

On the Sunday when he'd turned up unexpectedly, he promised to break up with his live-in girlfriend. When he'd got back after spending the day with me, he told her it was over between them. She had gone ballistic and thrown him out. Luckily for him, his tenant had done a runner. Well, not lucky really, as she owed him a month's rent. On the bright side, at least he had somewhere to go. She had left a mess, which Paul had to sort out, he was working out a plan to get the money that she owed him. Trust me, he would get it, I've learned since that nobody rips Paul off and gets away with it. Paul is like a detective; he gets a kick out of sniffing around other people's business. After a couple of weeks, he did indeed get his rent, with interest. God knows what he had said to her to get that, though he doesn't mess around. I felt that he had a bit of a dark side to him, in fact, I didn't like it really. However, I thought nobody is perfect and if that was his only fault, I could live with it. How wrong could I be! During our many conversations, I'd told Paul about my predicament and how urgent it was that I find somewhere else to live now. Although I was being careful, not suggesting anything rash, he kept saying I could move in with him. I thought it was way too soon to that, I didn't want to get too involved. He was extremely persistent and when I only had two weeks left at the flat, I began to think it may not be a bad thing. Time was running out for me, I had to sort myself out and get out of the flat. I didn't have many options and money was tight. Paul was kind, he appeared to genuinely care about me. I was at rock bottom; I had lost everything.

I couldn't get a grip on the kids' situation, I felt completely helpless about it. I needed somebody to help me to get back on my feet, I thought maybe Paul could do that. It was coming up to Christmas, I had agreed to be out of the flat the day after Boxing Day, for Billy to move back in. Not a great time for moving house, though Christmas was never a good time for me anyway in those days. Since leaving the kids, I never got to see them at Christmas, they always stayed at home with Donovan. Boxing Day was always spent with his family, there was no discussion or compromise, which was the way it was. I just had to deal with it. It got harder every year, I just cried my way through Christmas and got through it the best way I could. I didn't really want to see anybody as I didn't want to be a mood hoover, Christmas is all about happy family gatherings and I couldn't be happy. How could I be without my children? There is, a hundred percent, nothing worse. I was constantly grieving for them; it broke my heart every time I had to take them home. I just couldn't get over leaving them.

I was really down; I decided to go and see a clairvoyant. Everybody recommended Mrs Driver, this well-known lady in Hackness. Although I've always been a bit dubious about this sort of thing, I just needed some hope to cheer me up. I wondered if anything might be said to help me decide whether or not I should go ahead regarding moving in with Paul. There was no chemistry on my part with Paul, I didn't fancy him at all. I needed to be sure about this move before I agreed. The next Saturday afternoon, I was on my way to see the spook. I didn't have a wedding ring on, and I didn't want to give anything away, I didn't want to give her any clues about me at all. I knocked apprehensively on her front door and was greeted by a lovely old lady, with a shock of white hair, she was very similar to my mother, cuddly and she wore glasses, too. I liked her immediately as she made me feel safe and like everything was going to be okay.

Straightaway Mrs Driver picked up that I was not with my children. I broke down, kicking myself as I really didn't want to give the game away. I couldn't help it, whenever anyone talked to me about the kids and the way I was forced to leave them I would just end up crying. She reassured me that I had done the right thing, she said if I hadn't, I wouldn't have survived that marriage. He was a bad man, he would have killed me without a doubt if I had stayed, she said I had no choice and I had to stop feeling guilty. How did she know all this?

She continued the reading, saying that I had to stop blaming myself, everything would get better for me. She saw me moving to a place overlooking fields in the Selby area. What the actual fuck? She was describing Paul's flat. I hadn't been to see it at that time, I didn't know whether she was right or not, *how on earth did she know that?* My flabber was totally gasted. I was so intrigued. It was like she was reading the script of my life. Next, Mrs Driver said that I would meet someone who used to fly Aer Lingus and was in the forces. What!!! That was Paul as well. She was very specific, and the detail was weird. I couldn't believe what I was hearing. She went on to describe the man in my life now and said that he was not my usual type, though that wasn't a bad thing, I had gone for the wrong one before. He was a complicated character, yet he was a good person. It would be up to me how the relationship would go. I would be in charge. He would feel more for me than I did for him.

Mrs Driver talked about the kids next, saying that they were going to be okay, only she saw that one of them had a few health issues, they were going to be alright and that one of them would travel the world. She didn't say which one, she wasn't sure. That upset me again. I took it all with a huge pinch of salt. On the downside, she told me that my dad wasn't very well, he wasn't long for this earth, which upset me so much, I hadn't a clue, I burst into tears again when I heard that, I wasn't close to my dad, though I couldn't bear the thought of losing him. She said that my Mum wasn't a well lady either, though she would be okay, she had many years ahead of her. Despite having a problem with her heart, Mum would live to a good age.

How could she know all that? I was blown away. I had been concerned about my dad, he had been complaining about neckache and pain down the back of his arms. My Mum was just ignoring him, saying he was making a big deal of it. She wasn't very sympathetic with him at all. I felt sorry for him. Mrs Driver went on to say she saw another child in my life and that I would have three children. I dismissed that completely, no way. I didn't think that would happen at all. She said as far as work was concerned, I was going to be a successful PA and would "go higher". That was very encouraging.

Anyway, I left the house feeling very positive, thankful that Mrs Driver had reassured me that I was going to be okay. I felt very emotional and was exhausted from all the blubbing outbursts, yet I was so pleased I went to see her, she was absolutely bang on about my past and seemed to portray a great future for me. She was amazing. I believed everything Mrs

Driver told me as my life hadn't exactly been normal so far, she surely must have some sort of special powers to be able to read my life that specifically. Thank God as I couldn't see beyond the next couple of days at that point. There was a lot of positivity there, plus some not so positives, particularly about my dad, but I felt good when I left her.

I decided I would take the risk and move in with Paul. I wasn't happy working as a temp in Hackness and thought there may be some work for me in the Tankarsley area, or even Leathley. Who knows? For the first time in ages, I felt positive and believed that things were going to get better. I had nothing to lose – again! Paul came over that night. I decided not to tell him about the spook. He was really sceptical about things like that, I didn't want him to think that I had only agreed to move in with him because she more or less told me to, or it had been written in my script! We agreed that he would collect me on Boxing Day, I would start my new life with him. He was over the moon! Although I had my doubts and was a bit nervous about it, I was excited, too, as it would be a new start for me, away from Hackness and all the bad memories I had there. That was a good thing.

Paul had told me that his flat was a studio apartment. Well, when I got there, it was more like a bedsit. It was tiny. It was on the top floor of a small-town house. The stairs were really steep and when you got to the top of the stairs you were immediately in the lounge, which had a very small kitchen unit on the side of it, the bedroom was on the right, it literally just had a double bed in it with a tiny rail with a curtain covering the hanging space, not even a proper wardrobe. The interesting thing was when I looked out of the lounge window, there were nothing except fields for miles. Exactly what the spook had predicted.

I shuddered when I looked across the fields. If she was right about that, she must be right about everything else. I felt comforted by that, believing that I had done the right thing. After I got over the shock of the size of the flat, I made the best of it. We settled in. I didn't have any other choice really. Paul had definitely been economical with the truth as far as the size of the flat was concerned. The place needed sorting out. Soon after I moved in, I remember waking up one morning and feeling something fall on my face. When we looked up there was a flock, not sure if that is what you would call them, a load of ear wigs above on the ceiling, and they were dropping off down onto the bed. Oh, sweet lord, this place needed fumigating. I couldn't stand that. I sprayed them all with bleach, then ripped all the sheets off the bed. My skin felt like the little creatures were crawling on it, I was itching from head to foot. How awful. Paul just shrugged it off and laughed. After all he had lived in holes in the ground and probably eaten bloody ear wigs for his breakfast when he was in the forces. Things like that didn't bother him at all. I was freaked out. We managed to fumigate the room and get rid of them, thank God. After that incident, I never slept with my mouth open and clamped my mouth shut before I went to sleep.

I thought it was about time the kids met Paul. I was due to see them the following weekend. I knew that there wasn't room for them to come and stay in the flat and that really wasn't an option anyway, instead we arranged to pick them up and take them out for lunch the next Saturday. We turned up in Paul's red soft top car. It was a four-seater and the kids loved it. They climbed in the back and were delighted; it was like a fairground ride for them. Donovan looked quite jealous as he stood at the door. Just before we pulled away, Paul said that he would be having a word with Donovan when we dropped the kids off. I wondered what he meant by that, it couldn't be anything serious, I dismissed it and thought nothing more of it, I just wanted to have a nice time with the kids. They seemed to take to Paul quite well. Sarah was a bit dubious and very quiet. She just kept looking at him. Sizing him up. Tyler was fine, chatting away to Paul. The car was a real ice breaker though as they loved it. They both raised their hands in the air as we whizzed along the roads.

We took them to the flat, when we walked in, they both looked at each other and made comments about how small it was, I think they were hoping I had a big enough place for them to stay, I felt like I had let them down, again. I told them that if they wanted to come, we could sort something out. I never wanted them to think that I didn't want to have them overnight, or I didn't want to see them. Ever. That was paramount to me. We had a lovely day, went for lunch, came back via the park and then we took them back to Donovan's house. They rushed in and went straight out the back door to play on the street. They had had a lovely day. For the first time, I didn't feel terrible when I dropped them off, I knew they wanted to see me and that I would see them again, as soon as I could. Donovan was in the lounge, Paul told me he wouldn't be a minute he was just going to have a word with him. I waited in the hallway. It made me nervous being in the house, I just wanted to leave as quickly as possible. I listened at the door and heard Paul telling Donovan that he couldn't mess around with arrangements anymore, as there would be consequences if he did. Donovan opened the lounge door and told us both to leave. Paul suddenly got this wild look in his face, his eyes turned black, he bolted towards Donovan and pushed him up against the wall.

Paul said, "I know exactly what you did to her, and you won't be pushing her around anymore!"

When he let go of Donovan I could see my ex-husband was terrified. We turned and left. I didn't really know how to take that episode. Part of me felt good that someone had finally stood up for me, though part of me felt it was a mistake. I didn't know Paul was going to do that, if he had told me I would have told him not to do it. I didn't think that it was going to help me, as it turned out it didn't.

Donovan refused to let me have the kids the next time I was due to see them and when I called to confirm it, he just said, "You are living with a lunatic, you can't seriously expect me to let you have the kids when you are with him can you?"

I couldn't believe it or, actually, yes, I could. In a way I suppose he was right, Paul had made a huge mistake, I was angry that it had cost me my time with the kids. He did apologise, explaining to me that he had done it to help me and for the right reasons. He pointed out that Donovan was in the wrong, not him. Meanwhile, I wondered how the hell I was going to get things back on track with Donovan. I agreed that I would see the kids on my own, if that's what it would take for us to get things back to normal. Paul insured me on his car, I could use it now to pick them up. Donovan just put the phone down on me, this carried on for a couple of months. I was going insane not seeing the kids, I was worried about what they were thinking, or worse, what they were being told. I talked to them on the phone, which was always a strain, I just felt like I was constantly firing questions at them, and they couldn't wait to get off the phone. What a bloody mistake. I was livid with Paul, but I had to let it go.

Paul was still working as a lorry driver and a picker in a local factory. He was a Team Leader, though a useless one. He didn't get on too well with his fellow workers as he was quick to jump to conclusions, thinking they were plotting against him. They weren't, of course. Paul was starting to show signs of paranoia. Soon after I moved in, I landed a part time job as a medical secretary at the local GP's Surgery. Everything was moving to electronic records, most of my job was to scan medical records and save them to the files. Oh my God, it was boring. Thankfully it was only 9 am until 3 pm, which was enough for me, it was brain numbing. I didn't really connect with any of the staff either, they were all older than me and we had zero in common. As a couple of them knew Paul's ex, they took an instant dislike to me. Great. One of the girls told me that apparently Paul was engaged to this girl. He must have forgotten to tell me that! No wonder she kicked him out, she was gutted. She was busy planning their marriage, while he was busy planning his escape. That unnerved me slightly, though I gave him the benefit of the doubt after some of the things he had told me about her and the way she was.

We eventually managed to start seeing the kids again, only on a daily visit basis, and it was still very hit and miss, it had to be on Donovan's terms. Although it was difficult, it was better than nothing. One week, around Christmas time there was a pantomime on locally, we decided to take the kids. I booked the tickets, we picked them up from home and off we went. Tyler kept saying he didn't feel well and fell asleep in the car on the way over there. When we got to the pantomime, we all got our sweets and sat down. Tyler was sitting next to me. Within minutes of the curtain going up, he was asleep again. The noise coming from the stage was deafening, I couldn't understand how he could fall asleep with such a racket going on. He was as white as a sheet, too. I was seriously worried about him. I looked at Paul and pointed to Tyler.

Paul jumped up out of his seat and said, "Come on, we are taking him to the hospital, something isn't right, he shouldn't be sleeping through this noise."

We woke Tyler up, which wasn't easy, then whizzed off to the local A&E department. We didn't have to wait long before the doctor came to ask Tyler a load of questions, all of which my son couldn't really answer. I told the doctor I was his mother, I was ashamed to say I didn't live with him, so I wasn't sure how long he had been feeling as bad as he was. I told the doctor that he had been complaining for a while of feeling tired and sometimes having a sting in his wee, though when he had told his dad, he just reassured Tyler that it was only growing pains and nothing to worry about. The doctor was stunned and angry. So was I. He had taken a urine sample, when he brought it back, he said Tyler had an acute kidney infection and his wee was like Lucozade. He told me that Tyler needed to get to his own GP as soon as possible, as he needed to be referred to see the kidney specialist. I was absolutely horrified. I was livid with Donovan for ignoring Tyler, just burying his head in the sand for such a long time. The doctor told me to get Tyler in to see his GP the next day. In the meantime, the doctor gave him a strong antibiotic, told me to make sure Tyler drank loads of water to flush out the infection. The doctor reiterated that it was a very bad infection, it must have been going on for a while to get that bad. I felt really embarrassed and ashamed. I was his mother, and he was in such a state.

The doctor was very nice though I am sure he thought I was lying, that I had been neglecting my son. I wanted to scream I was furious with Donovan. We took him and Sarah straight home. When Donovan opened the door, I flew at him.

I told him what had happened and made him promise to take Tyler to his doctor first thing in the morning. He just said that Tyler had been complaining for a long time, he had just got used to it, and he thought Tyler was attention seeking, surely it can't be that bad. I was beside myself with rage and I could hardly speak. How could Donovan be such a stupid, thoughtless and selfish jerk. That's our son, for fuck's sake. I said my goodbyes to the kids, and we left.

I rang the next day to make sure Donovan had taken Tyler to the doctor. He said he had got an appointment for later that day. Thank God. I told him to let me know what the GP said. Of course, he didn't, I had to ring again that night. The doctor told Tyler to continue on with his antibiotics, he would refer him to a kidney specialist. He also queried Tyler's hearing ability. He thought that Tyler was having trouble hearing him. I had noticed this as well, I thought it was Tyler being quiet. The GP arranged for a hearing test, saying that he would make an urgent referral to the kidney specialist as well. Donovan just commented that it was a fuss about nothing, he was sure that Tyler would be fine. I told him to keep me informed, though I didn't expect him to do it. Tyler carried on struggling through school. He wasn't getting any help from Donovan or Julia, she continued to take care of the girls, excluding Tyler, even though he clearly wasn't well. Making him walk to school while the girls went in the car, waving as they went passed him. I was livid. Frustratingly, there was nothing I could do.

After a couple of weeks, Tyler received an appointment for the hearing test. I couldn't go as Donovan didn't tell me beforehand. Typical. Tyler's hearing had deteriorated, he was now going to need hearing aids. I had no idea. I wished to speak to the doctor to get the details, I called to do so. They were not allowed to speak to me, courtesy of Donovan's instructions. What the fuck. I was banging my head against a brick wall every time I tried to get information about my son's precious health. Donovan just kept minimising everything, saying that Tyler was going to have some hearing aids made for him. Exactly the same thing happened when Tyler's appointment to see the kidney specialist came through, I only found out after the appointment. Donovan deliberately didn't tell me, effectively, he stopped me from attending. As a result of Tyler's constant urine infections, hearing loss and lethargy, they decided to send Tyler to the hospital for a biopsy. They had linked the series of urine infections and the hearing loss together, concluding that he may have something called *Alport's Syndrome*, an extremely rare condition, which could result in renal failure. Eventually, Tyler would need a kidney transplant. I couldn't believe it or take it in.

I felt like I had let him down again. I was

beside myself. I just didn't want to believe it. My lovely son, Tyler, was going to have kidney failure... No, that couldn't be possible, I needed to know more about it. This time, I insisted that I speak to the specialist. To my surprise, I actually got through to him. He explained that this was a rare disease, not many people know that they have it. Sufferers can reach their early twenties and have kidney failure. In a way, Tyler was one of the lucky ones as he had started showing early signs of the disease, along with the deafness. This was also a sign. They had put two and two together and thought it was worth testing him for Alport's Syndrome. I asked the specialist how Tyler had got it, they said that it could happen at conception, or it could be that one of the parents was a carrier, usually the mother. I felt terrible again. It was my fault. I hadn't even been able to make Tyler properly. It was now confirmed that I was useless. Donovan would love that, something else to blame me for.

Soon after that Tyler went into a local Hospital where they did a biopsy on his kidney. It confirmed our fears that he did in fact have Alport's Syndrome. Tyler seemed to take it all in his stride though underneath I am sure he was terrified. It must have been devastating for 12-year-old Tyler to be told that his kidneys were going to fail, and he would need a transplant. He didn't talk about it much, he just seemed to accept it. God only knows what was really going through his mind. He must have been petrified and worried, instead of showing it, he just kept it all to himself. I struggled with this news, though when I tried to stay positive and talk to him about it, he would just clam up. His hearing continued to be monitored, as he was to receive regular check-ups on that, too. I had to trust Donovan to take Tyler to all the appointments as he assured me that he would. He didn't seem to understand what was happening, he just kept making light of it, totally burying his head in the sand whenever I talked to him about it. It was devasting for all of us, though I felt sorriest for Tyler and just wanted to help him. I wished it had been me with the illness, not Tyler. I would do anything to take it away from him. But there was nothing I could do at that time. We just had to make sure that he was monitored and kept his appointments. Any changes in his health had to be flagged up to the doctors.

At home, Paul and I were getting on well. When I woke up on Valentine's Day, he brought me a cup of tea with a small gift. I was surprised to find an engagement ring inside. I was blown away. I hadn't expected that, to be honest I wasn't sure if I wanted to take things that far with him. Paul had met my family a few times, they all found him a bit full on, although they thought he was a nice bloke. Apparently, one time we were at my Mum and Dad's house with the kids, when Paul disappeared with my dad into the garden and told him that I was with him now, he would be taking care of me. My Dad thought that was a bit odd, though he gave Paul the benefit of the doubt. Dina told me that Paul had done the same thing to her, she thought he seemed to be trying to convince everyone that we were a match made in heaven and he had been sent to take care of me. It was all a bit too much too soon. He had shown signs of becoming a bit possessive when we were with my friends, too.

When we had been to Hackness a few times, he saw that I knew quite a lot of people. He watched me like a hawk whenever anyone came over to talk to me, male or female. I always greeted people with a hug, I don't think he liked that. He didn't do that; he was not comfortable with hugging other people. One afternoon we bumped into Dylan from The Showroom. I hadn't seen him for ages, I was delighted to see him. We flung our arms around each other and kissed both our cheeks. When I turned to introduce Paul to Dylan, he had this wild look in his eyes and barged in between us. He moved Dylan away from me with one hand, telling him that I was with him now and to back off. Dylan just laughed it off, saying, "Alright mate", meanwhile I was horrified and told Paul to stop being so silly. Dylan was a good friend of mine. He raised his eyebrows behind

Paul's back at me, making signs indicating that Paul was a nutter. I just smiled though I was beginning to think he was right! I told Paul to calm down, reassuring him that he was just a good friend. He didn't seem to believe me. As far as Paul was concerned, if I hugged anyone it was because I fancied them, or they fancied me. Ridiculous. Due to this behaviour, I didn't know what to say when Paul presented me with the engagement ring. He was ecstatic. I didn't have the heart to disappoint him. I felt really sorry for him, if I turned him down, he would be absolutely gutted, I just didn't know what else to say apart from *yes*. If I had shown any signs of doubt, he may have turned funny on me and, after all, I had nowhere else to go.

Looking back now, I should have been stronger and told him it was too early, I realise these days that my default setting is always to try and make someone feel happy, of course, it's usually at my cost. I thought to myself just because we got engaged, it doesn't mean we have to get married. We could have a long engagement, then if things went pear shaped, we could just go our separate ways. Paul would get the reassurance he clearly needed and a bit of security with me. Yes, I really convinced myself that it was the right thing to do for both of us, that's why we went ahead with the engagement.

CHAPTER 15

A New-born Babe 1997

Paul was like the cat that got the cream once we were engaged. Weirdly, the ring he bought me was identical to the one Donovan had given me. The only difference was that the sapphire stone was a heart shape. He had never seen my first ring, as I'd pawned both of my rings shortly after the divorce from Donovan had come through. Actually, I needed the money, even though I was ripped off and only got £30 for both rings. I didn't want to keep them.

I really didn't imagine or expect that I would be engaged again and so quickly. It was not something I had wanted really, I convinced myself it was the right thing to do despite some of my misgivings about Paul. He was an odd person without a doubt, though I believed he was a good person, and he would take care of me. After all, there was no rule saying that if you get engaged you have to get married, I thought we could just drift along and stay engaged indefinitely.

We were on the hunt for a bigger place to live, I was desperate to have the kids to stay, especially now I knew about Tyler's health condition. I wanted to see more of them both and keep an eye on Tyler. I didn't trust Donovan at all to look after Tyler. He just couldn't seem to get a grip of Tyler's appointments and missed the odd one, his head was completely in the sand. He just wouldn't accept that Tyler had a very serious health condition. God knows I didn't want it to be true either, though it was happening, and we needed to do the best we could for Tyler and to take care of our son.

Anyway, Paul and I started to look at properties in the area. Everything we looked at was too much money. I had absolutely no money. I had received the funds from the endowment policy from my divorce with Donovan, it was only about £3,000. I'd been using it to survive when I was out of work sporadically, it had gone by then. I had signed my share of the house over to Donovan, on the agreement that he would stay in the house until the kids were both 18 and that my half of the house would go to them both.

From the minute we had moved into that house, Donovan always told me that he wouldn't leave it, I believed him. My main priority was that the kids stayed there as long as they were little and up until they both left school, I wanted to ensure that happened. There was no way I was going to push for him to sell the house to get my half of the proceeds, if it meant that the kids were going to have to move out and maybe live in a smaller place. It was of utmost importance to me that they stayed in that house. Besides, I knew I would survive somehow. As a result, I had no savings or any money for a deposit on a property by myself, or with someone else. Paul owned the flat, though it was mortgaged to the hilt, he would only just break even if he sold it. I think his dad had helped him buy the flat when he came out of the forces, as apparently his dad had moved by that time and there either wasn't room for Paul at their new property, or they didn't want him to live with them, most likely. Paul thought it would be a better idea for him to keep the flat, rent it out again, to give us some sort of income from that. It would help with the mortgage on a new property.

We racked our brains for a solution. After a while Paul decided he would ask his stepbrother Ronald if he could help us. He had properties all over the place and Paul thought it would be a good idea if we could rent one of those. He arranged for us to go and see Ronald. I felt extremely awkward as I knew the history of their relationship wasn't great, apparently Paul had been a pain in the arse by all accounts. I had a feeling it would be a complete wasted trip, I felt that Ronald wouldn't really want to help us. Why should he really? As Paul had almost broken Ronald's marriage, I thought it was a long shot, though Paul convinced me that it was worth a try. Ronald had a lovely big house nearby. We pulled up in the driveway like the poor relations, it was such a huge property, I immediately felt overwhelmed. I hadn't met Ronald or his wife, I was nervous about it. Ronald came to the door. I could see the awkwardness between him and Paul at once, though he was really nice to me and invited us both in. After a while Ampika, Ronald's wife joined us. She was really snobbish, looking down her nose at us both I just knew she didn't like Paul. She was polite to me, though I'm certain that she did not like me either. I could see the past still haunted her.

We made some polite conversation. I was actually dreading Paul asking Ronald for help. His way was crass, blunt and to the point. After about thirty minutes, he just blurted it out, asking Ronald if he had a property we could rent. Ronald nearly choked on his tea. Unfortunately, all of his properties were full at the moment he told him, due to that being the case, he couldn't help us. Typical. I knew it. What a bloody mistake. I felt incredibly stupid, as if I was a sponger.

Paul knew that there was an empty property round the corner from Ronald's house, he had driven past it on the way to there to check it out, that is why, he was sure. He asked about that one, Ronald told him that he had that earmarked for his son who would be moving in there soon. Ronald also said Ampika and himself would be moving soon to a large country house, the place with the aeroplane hangar, as he needed more space for his collection of cars.

Paul said, "Thought so," as he got that wild look in his eyes again.

Whenever he got angry his pupils would dilate and grow huge. He would do this really awkward smile and weird thing with his mouth, almost like a tick. It was really weird. Once he lost his temper, God knows what he would be capable of. Alarm bells rang. I told Paul that maybe it was time we left.

Paul just looked at Ronald, he said, "Thanks for nothing."

He kept staring at him. It was all really awkward. Despite Paul's stupid behaviour, Ronald was polite enough. As we left, Ronald looked me straight in the eye and wished me good luck. I said thanks and we left. So that was a no go. Back to the drawing board. We kept on looking around for somewhere suitable, though we didn't really get anywhere.

Paul spoke to Angus now and again. They were always really strained conversations that usually ended up with one of them slamming the phone down on the other. Angus was showing signs of illness, he told Paul that he had been falling over in the garden and losing his balance. I didn't like the sound of that. Paul didn't seem concerned, joking that he had been drinking too much. Angus didn't drink! Well, at least not anymore, he used to though I think it was getting out of control and he was fined for drink driving at one point as he raced around in one of his flash cars. Paul kept banging on about how loaded his dad was, it was a good idea for us to keep in touch with him, as maybe he would help us to buy a property. Paul used to throw out loads of hints when he spoke to him, Angus just didn't take the bait. It was embarrassing.

Paul was putting pressure on me to make things official, he wanted us to get married. He said it would help if his dad thought he had a wife to support. On top of that he said he had no doubt that I was the one for him from the minute he set eyes on me at the Club. I didn't feel the same. I couldn't admit that though. Funnily enough, Paul told me when we first met that he would grow on me. I thought that was quite sad really at the time. He knew that the feeling wasn't mutual, though I think he made it his mission to make me feel the same as him. He had a big heart and was very protective over me. I needed that at the time. He had his faults and sometimes he was hard work and often embarrassing, though I believed he loved me, I didn't have the heart to say no to him. I was weak, again. I just wanted security and somebody to take care of me.

When it came closer to the wedding, funds were running low as usual. There was no chance of a church wedding at that time as I had been divorced and with our financial pressures, we decided we should book in at Gretna Green. We had driven up there one day to see what it was like and thought it would be a different way of doing things. I would have liked a church wedding though I wasn't particularly excited about the wedding. Deep down I knew I was just going ahead with it for Paul's sake. We booked a 6 pm wedding slot over the anvil and thought that would give us all chance to get up there and would mean that we would only need to stay for one night. They offered a great package. There were a few rooms available, an evening meal and the ceremony all thrown in, the downside was there would be about six other couples all celebrating in the evening in the same room. It was a bit like marrying in bulk! It didn't bother me really as we only really had my close family to invite, Paul's family wouldn't be there, he didn't really want them to come.

Angus was too old and far away to make the trip, Ronald made some excuse that they were going to be away that weekend, that's why I thought the other couples and their guests would fill the room up for us and create a great atmosphere, we'd have a good knees up. We arranged a minibus to take us all up there, Donovan even agreed to let Tyler and Sarah come and stay the night. We took my Mum and Dad, Dina, Paddy and the kids, Harry,

Tyler, Sarah and Little Eileen, my friend from the post office, came, too. Carol couldn't make it as she had the kids to look after. Paul was the driver, he was in his element, being in charge and at the wheel. I wore a black velvet off the shoulder evening dress, carried yellow roses and wore some in my hair. Paul wore a kilt, he looked really good. He brushed up quite well, however, if I'm being honest, I still didn't fancy him! I was in too deep now, though, I just kept thinking he would grow on me. Sometimes in certain light or from behind he did look quite attractive!

We all trundled up there in the morning and arrived in the middle of the afternoon. We all booked into our rooms; they were pretty basic though they would be okay. All the kids were in the same room, they had a ball. There was a games room, and they were playing pool and really enjoying themselves. They didn't see much of each other usually; it was good that they all got on. The service went by in a flash. It was a speedy service with zero hymns or anything like that. The piper played once we had made our vows. We moved into the evening reception quite quickly. That was it, I had done it again. To my surprise it actually felt good to be married again, I really hoped that I had done the right thing this time. I would say I was seventy five percent sure that I had. I still had my underlying doubts, though I pushed them to the back of my mind, I just got on with the wedding. It was a really good knees up, we all enjoyed it. Paul was in his element, I felt happy for him. He hadn't had much luck in his life. I really wanted him to be happy at last. He was.

We drove back the next day to spend a few days at home together. We couldn't afford to go away, though Paul didn't seem bothered about it, he'd done all his flying when he was in the RAF, he had no urge whatsoever to catch a plane to anywhere. We organised a trip to visit his dad in Somerset in a couple of weeks' time, we would call that our honeymoon. I was nervous about meeting his dad, after all that Paul had told me about him, he sounded like a right old devil. I decided to keep an open mind, take his dad as I found him, surely, he couldn't be as bad as Paul said, he was probably exaggerating.

A couple of weeks after the wedding, we arrived in Falmouth to stay for a weekend with Angus. I had never been to Somerset; I was stunned at how beautiful it was and how completely overwhelmed I felt when I saw the palm trees! I had never seen one before. There seemed to be huge pineapples all over the place, especially bang slap in the middle of their roundabouts. It was a lovely time of year, too, really hot weather, I absolutely loved it. What a fantastic place to live. Angus was exactly as I had imagined him to be. Extremely tall, he was a military man. He had a very long grey beard and a huge nose. His glasses looked like they had been integrated into the top of his nose. Angus loved wearing his hats, usually he wore a baseball cap. Other times, he'd wear his cowboy hat. He thought he looked something else in that one!

A three-bedded bedroomed bungalow was his home, full of old furniture, stuff piled everywhere, really untidy, even though he had a cleaner. Well, that's what we thought she did. Twice a week she would come to the house. Later, we found out that Angus had been paying her for sex. She would charge him £100 for a blow job, or £200 for a massage and a happy ending. Paul thought that was funny, though I did not, I thought it was disgusting. She was taking advantage of him. I didn't like that much. I'd been wondering why the house wasn't that clean, she was obviously trying to make more money and concentrating on the extras rather than keeping the place clean.

The first thing I did was give the kitchen the once over, then the bathroom, I wasn't going to use a dirty bathroom, not a chance. The awkwardness between Paul and his dad was really obvious. Almost every conversation was a disagreement, finishing with his dad telling me how Paul was a waste of space and I'd married such a useless article. Angus kept asking me why

I was foolish enough to marry Paul. Was there something I didn't know? Why was he so down on Paul? I couldn't understand it and stuck up for Paul whenever I could. Despite Angus being an arse, I did get on really well with him, mainly as I just humoured him by going along with most things he said. Very opinionated, Angus thought he was right about everything. He kept on asking me why the hell had I got involved with such a waster, though I would just laugh it off and tell him Paul would prove him wrong. He wasn't convinced.

We had a good old sniff around the area, I absolutely loved it, I had no idea such a beautiful place existed in our country. Why go abroad, when we have such lovely coastlines and places in Somerset. I was hooked. I couldn't wait to go back again. Paul was over the moon that I had taken to Somerset, especially that I had hit it off with his dad. The only downside to the visit was Paul's driving. It was a bit of a white-knuckle ride for such a long journey, he wasn't the most careful driver in the world, though we made it there and back in one piece. After the wedding and our trip to Somerset, I was starting to think about getting a fulltime job, maybe in Leathley, to help with the finances. BOOM! I began to feel really unwell. Sickly and tired. Yes, that's right, I was pregnant. I was shocked. Not part of the plan. I left it for a week or so before I took a test, I thought it could have been a bug I caught from working at the doctors, or at least I hoped it was. There was always something going around there. Nope. I was pregnant. Holy crap, what was I going to do about that? When I told Paul his reaction was typical. He just thought he was really clever; he didn't seem to be grasping the fact that we were going to have a real live baby! I was in a proper dilemma. There was no way I could get rid of it; I knew I would have to just go ahead and hope for the best.

As I was now thirty-six years old, I was worried that there may be some problems, being an older mother, especially as I'd done drugs and drank my way through the few months that I'd lived with Billy. What if I'd done myself some harm? As I was ashamed of what I'd done back then, I didn't want to tell the doctors about it, and I was still working there at the time. I just didn't want anyone there getting wind that I had been off the rails and on drugs. I kept that to myself, though I was very worried about it. After we got used to the idea of a baby coming, I decided to stay working part time at the doctors until after the baby's birth. I could think about what to do afterwards. I told one of the doctors that I was worried about the baby's health due to my age. He said that if I was seriously concerned, he could arrange a *Chronic Villus Sampling* (CVS) test for me, adding that it was risky and invasive, with a threat of miscarriage, yet it was the quickest way of testing for abnormalities.

Bearing in mind the stage of the pregnancy I was in by then; he would recommend it. Despite being extremely nervous about it, I agreed to go ahead with it. As selfish as it may sound, I knew there was no way on earth either of us could cope with a disabled baby. It would be better to find out now, as we could then do something about it, if necessary.

The doctor pulled some strings and got me in the next day for the test. After they gowned me up, the doctor told me there would be a needle inserted into the placenta and they would nip a piece away to take it for testing. Even though it all sounded a bit grim to me, I didn't think too much about it, it just had to be done. I still freaked out when the doctor came round the curtain, holding, what looked like to me, a bloody great big knitting needle. It must have been about a foot long! I really didn't like the thought of a needle going anywhere near the baby. I managed to convince myself that it was the best thing to do for all of us, including the baby. I went ahead, had the test, they told me after to relax and keep my feet up for the rest of the day. They would call me the next day with the results of the test. I was terrified. What if there was a problem? What would we do, as there was no way I wanted to get rid of it, though, equally, I knew damn well that I would end up on my own to struggle along with a disabled child if there was anything wrong?

Paul would hundred percent *not* be able to cope with that. What a bloody predicament. It was a long night.

They called me about lunchtime the next day, announced that everything was fine, we were having a little boy. All his bits and pieces were intact, he was okay. Thank holy God for that. I was beyond relieved, really pleased that we had taken the risk of having the test and delighted that we were having a boy, too. We had not expected them to tell us the sex of the baby, we wanted a surprise, oh well, now that was blown! However, the main thing was that our son was healthy and okay. I was about fourteen weeks pregnant at that time, if there had been a problem, another week and I would have had to give birth if we had decided to abort. I was thankful to God that everything was fine.

Several weeks later, I began to get horrendous pains around my pubic area, they were excruciating when I walked, even when I was lying down, I was in pain. I could hardly bear it. I was really struggling to walk anywhere. I told the doctor and he sent me for an Xray. The photo showed that I had a split pubic symphysis bone. Apparently, it was quite rare, due to the pressure of the baby on my pubic bone. It was bloody agony. I got to the stage where I was crying with the pain. Nothing seemed to help it, I couldn't sit, walk, stand, or lay down for very long. The doctor signed me off work, telling me to have complete bed rest. Consequently, my time with the kids became limited. Paul said he would go over and collect them to bring them over to see me, however, Donovan wasn't keen on that. Every time we tried to arrange it, he'd say the kids were busy or they just simply refused to come over. I didn't see either of them for the last couple of months of that pregnancy. We had to give up on our search for a new house, though I knew the flat was way too small, I would be struggling to get a pram or a pushchair up and down those bloody stairs. We needed to get somewhere else to live, pronto, preferably before the baby came along. We managed to get ourselves added to the urgent list for a council house or flat. We had a visit from the council, once the lady saw the tiny flat and the stairs, she pulled a few strings. She told us that she would expedite our application, which meant that we would get something very soon after the baby was born. I told her we would take anything the council could offer, as we needed to get out of that flat we were living in. The pain from the pubic problem was getting worse by the week, the heavier the baby got the worse it was, I felt like my body was splitting in two, it was like having constant period pains though it was even worse than that. It was agreed with the doctor that I would be taken into hospital two weeks before the due date, as there was no way I could go through the pain of the early stages of labour on top of the pain I was already going through. I was worried in case I had a quick labour, and they would not have time to give me any pain relief, I couldn't bear the thought of that. Although I didn't want to spend too long in the hospital, I just knew it would be the only safe way of doing dealing with this situation. I still enjoyed feeling the baby moving around, it absolutely fascinated me, just as it did with Tyler and Sarah, despite the pain I was constantly in.

I went into hospital two weeks before, as planned. Not much to do, but lay in the bed, waiting. It was pretty boring, though Paul came in to see me every evening. I was really missing Tyler and Sarah, I was worried that they may be feeling pushed out, perhaps they would be thinking that I didn't want to see them. There was nothing I could do, I just couldn't get to see them unless they were allowed to come to see me by their father, and he wasn't helping.

I just had to live with that and pray that it wouldn't make things even more difficult the next time they saw me, especially with a new brother for them to get used to. I was booked in for an epidural to help me with the pain. Thank God. I started showing early signs of labour on the due date again. That happened with all three of my children. Bang on the dates. That's unusual I was told. Anyway, I alerted the nurses as soon as I felt the pains, they took me to the delivery suite to get prepared and gave me an epidural. It only seemed to be working on my right side, though it was enough to dull the pain and, thankfully, Owen came into the world on 21 May 1997. He was a good size, 8llb 2oz such a cute little baby. A tinge of ginger adorned his fine hair, though I ignored that. He was gorgeous, I was over the moon to meet him. Paul made it for the birth, though only just, he had been at work, and they didn't give him long to get there. I wouldn't have been bothered really if he hadn't been there, I felt all the way through the pregnancy that Paul was just going along with it, he didn't seem to be particularly excited about having a son. He didn't ask to hold him and when I offered to hand Owen to him, Paul backed off, saying, no, he would rather wait until we got him home.

Paul didn't have a clue about babies, he had never had anything to do with them, he'd never been near one, as far as I knew. It wasn't really surprising then, that Paul didn't know how to hold his son. I felt sorry for him though, in a way, I was pleased that it was the opposite way around to when I had given birth to Tyler when he had been taken away from me and glued to Donovan for the first precious hours. I was still in Hospital and once I had recovered from the birth, I was desperate for the kids to meet their new baby brother.

After a couple of days, Paul told me that he would go over and collect Tyler and Sarah to bring them to the hospital to see Owen and me. I was very excited; I could hardly wait. I hoped and prayed that they would be delighted and not jealous or feel awkward about it all. When they walked in, they both looked really timid. They came over to me and at first didn't seem to notice Owen in the cot next to me, they sat on the bed. I pointed at Owen, saying to them, meet your brother. Then they both went over to him and peered in the cot. Sarah didn't seem too bothered, it was a baby, yay! She was not that impressed. Tyler just found him funny, bursting out laughing at Owen. He thought he was cute though, apparently, not cute enough for Tyler to hold his brother. Neither of them wanted to hold Owen. I think they were both overwhelmed, we hadn't seen each other for about two months, and it seemed to have taken its toll on us. I just felt like I was firing questions at them that they were reluctant to answer.

After about an hour, Paul announced that Donovan had told him that Tyler and Sarah needed to be back home by teatime, it was time for him to drive them home and we would see them again once I was out of hospital. They were so quick to leave, I felt deeply sad after they had gone, as I could feel the distance between us, I just wondered what they were both thinking.

I had to stay in hospital for another week until my pubic bone had gone back into its usual position. It was still painful though nowhere near as bad as it was when it had Owen's head pushing on it! The doctors told me I would not be capable of carrying any more children, part of me thought thank God! I didn't want to go through that pain ever again. It was savage. Owen was adorable. Such a quiet, lovely, little boy. I breastfed him, as I had done with Tyler and Sarah, and I loved it. We were inseparable. I would carry him around all the time, I never wanted to let him go. Paul was better with him when we got back to the flat, he would spend time cuddling him at night when he finished work. Paul really started to bond with him, too, in his own way, though he used to enjoy watching me with Owen. He told me that seeing me and Owen together and how much I loved him, had made him realise just how hard it must have been for me having to leave Tyler and Sarah. Paul could see how much Owen meant to me. He promised me that there was no way that I would ever be separated from Owen. He said he would never dream of doing that to me, he couldn't understand how Donovan could have done it to me. If only that were true.

CHAPTER 16

Suspicious Mind 1998

While Paul was out at work, I loved to take Owen out for a walk, though it nearly killed me to drag the pram up and down those steep old stairs. My baby son would be gurgling away, as I pushed him round the streets. For the first time in ages, I felt contented and happy. I did my best to stay in touch and to see Tyler and Sarah as much as I could. As usual, Donovan was making that as difficult as ever. I am convinced that he was saying stuff, like, *'now your mum has that new baby, she won't be interested in you'*. I believe that sort of thing was pretty much guaranteed, I was sure of it. I just had to see them when I could and hope to convince them otherwise and keep in touch with them regularly. I missed them so much.

After a while I found out that Donovan and Julia had got married. Donovan must have forgotten to tell me that. He had told the kids not to tell me. God knows why, that should have been something he wanted to shout from the rooftops, not keep it a secret. Apparently, it was a really quiet wedding, a bit similar to ours, very low key, just close family invited. I'd met Julia a couple of times when I had dropped the kids off, she seemed nice enough, she was very small with ginger hair and didn't seem to match her kids, who were all very dark haired and two of them were quite tall. I thought that was a bit odd. Maybe her ex was tall and Italian! I don't know. She had received quite a large settlement from her divorce, she had bought a three bedroomed house with it. Donovan had refused to move in there, as they agreed that she would sell her property, then she and her family would move into Donovan's house. I was glad to hear that, as part of our divorce settlement was conditional on Tyler and Sarah staying in that house until they were both eighteen, I would have been gutted if he had broken that promise. Tyler hated it. I don't think Tyler wanted them to get married. Tyler clearly didn't get on with Julia, the thought of her becoming his stepmother wouldn't be a great idea as far as he was concerned. As he was very loyal to his dad, he just had to go with it. Donovan had made his mind up, that was the end of it. The house was cramped and full of girls, what a nightmare for Tyler. He was still struggling, still being ignored and made to walk to school, even though he felt like shit. Sarah was happy, she had inherited three sisters, who got on really well with one another, they became quite close. Sarah and the girls were pretty much inseparable, she loved spending time with them.

I felt really sorry for Tyler as he was being pushed out. He took a liking to his new brother, Owen, he used to sit with him on his knee, showing much more interest in him than Sarah did back then. Tyler had always found babies amusing and liked them. He could make Owen giggle and that made him laugh. Tyler and laughing didn't happen often, when it did his whole face absolutely lit up. He had such a lovely face and smile. Sarah didn't seem interested in Owen at all, not sure if that was hidden jealousy, or she just simply didn't care! Never know with Sarah.

It was a rocky marriage, by all accounts, between Donovan and Julia. Remarkably, it sounded like Julia was the one in charge and not Donovan. I saw one of their neighbours on the street, she told me that she heard some humdinger rows, things were being thrown around. A bit like when I was there, though it was me that was being flung around, not household objects! In a way that made me feel good, what goes around comes around, I thought to myself. It seemed their marriage was no happier than mine had been with him. However, I didn't like the sound of things being chucked around, especially if the kids were in the house. I had always done my best to protect them from that sort of thing, I certainly didn't want that going on in their lives. Donovan had always wanted the house full of kids, now he had his wish with five of them living there. I don't think he even noticed that Tyler was struggling, feeling so pushed out. Donovan was just concentrating on keeping Julia and the girls happy, never mind about his son.

Tyler formed a band with some school mates, it was going well. He was becoming really popular and well known for his unique drumming skills. He had a natural talent. Even though he was quiet at school, he was becoming very popular. They would practise after school and Tyler spent most of his free time drumming. He loved it, he was clearly extremely talented as he couldn't read music, yet he seemed to be able to play anything. Tyler was becoming a gifted drummer. I was proud of him. My mum was a self-taught pianist, sometimes she played a bit like Les Dawson, though she was a pianist in a local ballet school in the past. I think she was a pretty good musician, most of the time. She always takes the credit for Tyler's musical talent. Perhaps it does come from her, who knows.

I was constantly on the phone to the council, trying to get news of a bigger house for us. Paul seemed to have given up, I think he would have been quite happy to stay at his tiny flat. Once again, I was hoping we would get something with a spare room, then we could have the kids to stay over, and we'd all be together. That would have been a dream come true for me. I kept pushing them for a three bedroomed place, I made sure they knew that I had three children. Eventually, they offered us a two bedroomed flat. They didn't seem to care about me being separated from my kids. We went to look at the flat. It was in a really lovely village. It reminded me of my childhood village and those hot happy summer days when I was little. I was pleased, as I thought we were very lucky to be offered something in such a lovely area. Even though it was quite small to us, it was much bigger than Paul's flat. We signed on the dotted line and took it. I couldn't physically wait to get out of that pokey flat. It was becoming a real struggle. There was stuff everywhere and I can't stand mess.

The place was ideal, though, of course, it needed to be decorated. The paintwork was rubbish, with the wallpaper peeling off the walls. Paul's brother, Ronald, got wind that we were moving near to him, not sure how, though I had a feeling that Paul had made sure he knew. Anyway, Ronald offered to send some of his lads round to decorate it for us before we moved in, he said it could be a belated wedding present. I couldn't believe it. I was delighted and so grateful to him for that. Especially knowing how he felt about Paul. We arranged to meet

Ronald at the flat and I chuckled to myself when he pulled up outside, as he turned up in one of his classic cars! A few curtains twitched when Ronald smirked as he got out of the car and walked up the garden. He had quite a presence about him and was a powerful character. Paul looked really jealous, he just tut tutted, saying that it was typical of Ronald to make a big entrance. I didn't care, I thought it was quite funny. Anyway, we went through some colour schemes, and he told me I could choose any colours I wanted. He spotted that the carpets were knackered, and he offered to throw in new carpets throughout for us, too. I couldn't believe it. Even though he would probably put it all through on his business account, I thought he was very generous, I was grateful for his help. I was over the moon; I couldn't thank Ronald enough and I walked with him out to the car. Just before he left, I thanked him again.

Ronald looked at me and said, "You deserve it, living with a plonker like Paul."
I didn't reply.

He continued, "I just wanted to help you and Owen."

I wasn't sure what to say to that, though deep down I couldn't help but agree with him. I thought that was a very weird thing to say but, hey, we got the place decorated for nothing, I wasn't going to complain. Ronald told me they would do it within a few days, he would call me when it was finished. We were still able to stay in the other flat until it was ready, I preferred to do that as I didn't want to be living there with Owen while they were painting. It was lovely when we moved in, they had done an amazing job, it was bright and fresh. Owen's room was spacious, decorated in blue and yellow, it was a lovely bright and happy room for him. The carpets were super bouncy, they were the same in every room, I loved it. Finally, we had some space, though still not enough room to have Tyler and Sarah staying over. I was disappointed, my efforts on that front appeared to be doomed, as everywhere I'd lived since, I'd left their dad, just did not have room for them. I couldn't catch a break on that situation at all. I hoped and prayed that they didn't think it was the way I wanted things to be, as it certainly was not. We settled in quickly within a week or two. As we didn't have too much stuff, it was an easy move for us. After a struggle to get a tenant in Paul's flat, he decided he wanted to get rid of it and he put it on the market. Nobody seemed to be in interested in it. Paul didn't seem bothered, he kept saying it would sell eventually and as he wasn't going to make any money out of it, he was in no real rush. He would most likely just about break even on it.

Paul was in touch with his dad now and again, though not as often as I was. Angus started to call me when Paul was at work more often than he rang Paul. He'd chat away about nothing, moan about the neighbours and telling me how many times he'd fallen over that day. He kept bumping into things around the house, too, and though he made nothing of it, I was worried, it didn't seem right at all. His cleaner was coming in still, though whether she was actually doing any cleaning would be another matter. I didn't like to think about that. It still annoyed me that she was ripping him off. That wasn't right. Paul just kept saying I was doing a good job, I should keep it up, we may inherit something if I kept in with his dad. Honestly, that was not the reason I was keeping in touch with Angus, he was Paul's Dad, Owen's grandad, he didn't have anyone else in his life. He was family. The last thing on my mind was inheriting anything, I just felt sorry for Angus, I wanted to help him if possible.

Paul was very materialistic, he kept saying his dad owed him big time after the way he treated him when Paul was a child. To a certain extent, I agreed with that, though as time passed, Angus was an old man now, living on his own. Whatever he'd done in the past, he didn't deserve to be struggling on his own. Paul was extremely emotionally detached, he didn't seem to have any feelings for his dad, apart from the belief that his dad owed him something. We definitely didn't have that in common. At that time, Paul was working at the factory in Tankarsley. He kept getting into trouble, due to the fact that he was very suspicious of people, he fell out with the other members of his team. People started to complain about his behaviour. I told him to stop looking for trouble, he should just get on with his job and let other people be. However, it was in his nature to be suspicious of people. He couldn't seem to help it.

During that time, I stayed at home with Owen as long as we could afford it, as I loved being around him, he was such a good baby. I had met a lovely girl called Evangeline, who lived in a quirky cottage, ex council, she had bought it. Her house was in the corner of the estate nearly opposite to our place. It was a magical house, very calm and zen like. I had seen Evangeline walking to and from the school. Her long jet-black hair was stunning, she was a striking looking woman, she was beautiful. Yolanda, her daughter, went to the local primary school. One day, when Evangeline was walking past, I was in what you may call a bit of a front garden with Owen, when she came over to say hello to us. She loved Owen; she was really good with him. He giggled at her. I could tell she was really kind, a lovely person. We clicked straightaway. She asked me to pop over for a bowl of homemade soup the next day and after that we started to see each other quite regularly.

She was quite bohemian, with her floaty tops and white linen outfits. Ged, her live in boyfriend, was like the male version of her, with the same length, long, black hair. It was weird. From behind they looked like a pair of twins. They'd met in the local pub, falling for each other straightaway. Evangeline told me she used to shake when he came to sit beside her as her feelings for him were so strong. Ged was ten years younger than her, though they both looked about the same age to me. What a great couple. Ged was musical, he played the guitar. Although he was a bit of a rocker to look at, he was a lovely bloke, easy going, friendly and a bit on the shy side. He was a clever and worked at Barclays Bank in Leathley. Paul and I became great friends with them both. We would pop in and out of each other's homes for cups of tea and lovely homemade cakes or soup! Evangeline used to work in the evenings selling mortgages, she was good at it. She had such a way with people. She was warm and had such a great aura, everyone instantly got on with her.

Paul always had a big ego, he kept saying Evangeline fancied him, which was ridiculous. Oh well, he thought any woman that smiled at him fancied him. I got used to that, I just laughed to myself. We would go into town for the odd night out, Evangeline and I used to leave the boys at the bar and dive onto the dance floor as soon as we got there. We had great fun, running around the club holding hands! She was a wonderful friend to me. I cared about her very much. She offered to help out with

Owen whenever we needed any help, as she was at home most days. Owen really liked her. I started to think about getting another job. As Paul had fallen out with almost everybody at his job in Tankarsley, he had shifted jobs to another factory in South Milford, doing more or less the same thing, except now he was working night shifts, with not as much contact with other people. It suited me, as he would go to work about 5pm and not come back until the early hours. It meant I had every evening to myself; I could spend loads of time on my own with Owen. I loved that. The money was better than his job in Tankarsley, though it was not really enough for all our needs. I would have to go back to work.

I didn't want to leave Owen and I thought I could get something to fit in with Paul's hours to save on childcare costs. I wasn't keen on leaving Owen with Paul, due to the fact that they had not spent a lot of time together before. Besides, Paul had no clue about how to look after Owen. I did it all. Anyway, I randomly picked a recruitment agency based in Leathley. I decided to give them a bell and I spoke to the manager, Rennie, she was brilliant. She was really good at her job, she made me feel like I was a super secretary and could get any job she sent me for. Rennie gave me so much confidence, it was ridiculous. I arranged to go into Leathley to meet her to register with the agency. We hit it off immediately, she knew exactly what I was looking for. Not long after that she placed me at a large Firm of Solicitors in Leathley, it was fulltime, though it came with a really good salary, I thought it was going to really sort us out. Perhaps we could start looking for a bigger place finally. I began commuting on the train from the local station into Leathley and Paul would look after Owen until 2pm, then, either Evangeline would have him until I got home, or I had managed to get him a place at a local nursery from 2pm to 6pm. Though the childcare was expensive, I didn't want to rely on Evangeline.

I enjoyed my new job in Leathley, I worked with some great people. We had such a laugh, it really did me good to get back in the real world for a few hours. I was mainly working on large documents, which I enjoyed. Paul was useless with Owen though, it worried me. We had a tropical fish tank in the lounge. I got home from work one day to find the carpet in there was completely soaked and stained. I wondered what on earth had happened, it stunk, too. I rang Paul at work, he told me that he had been cleaning the fish tank out and filling it back up with a hose pipe. He had left the pipe in the tank when, somehow, Owen had managed to get hold of it. He was swinging it around the room by the time Paul came back from chatting Evangeline up outside! What a plonker. I was furious, he hadn't cleaned it up properly, it absolutely stunk in there. That was typical of Paul, he easily forgot what he was doing and got distracted. What a nightmare!

When Evangeline and Ged were getting married, they invited us to the wedding. It was on a Friday. I took the day off, though Paul was unable to get the time off, which meant that we couldn't go. I wanted to be there to see them get married, I told Paul I was going to go. He wasn't happy about it. He didn't want people thinking I was single and hitting on me. What was he thinking, he had a one track, suspicious mind? I thought that was ridiculous and I stood my ground. I was going to go, whether Paul liked it or not. It was a lovely wedding in the local church, all the locals came out to see Evangeline in her dress, she looked absolutely stunning, they made such a great couple. Yolanda was a bridesmaid, she looked amazing, just like her mum. They were such a perfect little family. I couldn't have been happier for them. I was really glad that I went to the wedding. Paul told me that he might come for the evening bash, after he finished his shift. In a way, I hoped he wouldn't, as he was becoming more and more embarrassing, making stupid assumptions about people.

Paul turned up about 7:30pm, with that wild look in his eyes again, as he bolted straight over to me, to ask me who I'd been talking with. I told him to calm himself down and get a drink. This was a wedding, not a singles bar. I was enjoying sharing my dear friends' special day and I was determined that Paul was not going to be allowed to spoil it by making an unnecessary scene. He gave me a weird look, then went and stood at the bar. We got through it without incident, thank God, though he was watching me like a hawk all night. I just ignored him. He was being really paranoid and ridiculous. Why couldn't he just accept that when people talk to each other, it doesn't always mean that they want to shag each other. It was getting me down.

After a while, Paul changed his shifts at work, which cocked up my plans for Owen and my time alone with him, too. Due to Paul now working early shifts, I had to drop Owen at nursery early, then get the train into Leathley. Paul would pick Owen up from nursery when he finished work at 3pm, afterwards he'd drive into Leathley to pick me up from work at 5pm. I am convinced he was only doing it to check that I wasn't talking to anybody at work. He was always sitting in the downstairs car park when I came out, watching me like a hawk. If any blokes were walking out at the same time as me, he would quiz me about who they were. I was getting absolutely sick of it, though it was a lift home and saved me getting the train, plus I got more time to see Owen in the car on the way home, I just put up with it. It was almost as if he was convincing himself that I was cheating on him. God knows why, that's the last thing I would do. I was nothing more than friendly to anyone.

Sometimes, on a Sunday afternoon, my family came over, or we would go over to Hackness to see them. It was always difficult as I felt that they thought Paul was a nutcase. Nobody ever voiced it, I could just tell that they weren't sure about him. He was extremely possessive, and he would get the wrong end of the stick about things that were said. Family gatherings were few and far between due to Paul's ways. It was easier that way.

Over time, Angus was having more and more of his weird episodes. I was talking to him one day on the phone.

Angus asked, "Would you be prepared to come down to Somerset to take care of me, if anything happened to me?"

My heart went out to him, "Of course I would!"

"You don't stand a chance with a waster like Paul. I'd like to give you and Owen a start in life. Look, if you agree to look after me so that I can stay in my own home, you, Paul and Owen, you can all move in with me here. Then, when I pass on, I'll leave Paul the house, but really, it's for you and Owen, so you'll have a better life, Sophia."

"I don't know what to say. Angus, thank you, you're a good man," I felt choked up a bit.

"You'll be doing me a big favour, I don't want to go into a nursing home, I don't want to pay for that. I want to stay here in my own bungalow as long as I can. I know I'm not very well; I keep falling over, soon I won't be able to look after myself," he told me.

"Angus, I'll have to think about it," I said.

"What's there to think about? I know you love Somerset, Sophia, it's a good thing for Owen, you, Paul, and me."

However, it was not only my little Owen I had to think about, but I also had Tyler and Sarah, as well.

How could I leave them up North?

I couldn't be that far away from them. It just wouldn't be right. I wanted to help Angus, though I'd be lying if I said it wasn't tempting, the bungalow was lovely, it was in a gorgeous area. The problem was it would mean leaving my other two kids, and all my family and friends, and my job, which I enjoyed. I wasn't sure I could do that. When I told Paul, he acted as if we'd won the bloody lottery. He was overjoyed.

"There's no question, we should do it!" he told me, immediately, no thought needed for him.

It is what he had been waiting for.

I responded, "Paul, I need to think about it all, because I have all my family to consider and, most of all, Tyler and Sarah."

"Sophia, we hardly see them anyway, I think we should think about ourselves, you, me and Owen. We should go, as soon as we can!"

He was adamant about it. I was in such a dilemma. It was a great opportunity, for sure, though it would be me who would be paying the price, I would have to leave my Tyler and Sarah again. I didn't think I could do that to them. I needed to be near them, especially Tyler. Paul wouldn't hear of it. No conversation. Paul had made his mind up; we would do it. He didn't seem to give a shit about my kids or the way I was feeling about it. He just kept banging on about the house, his dad's money and his cars. I could almost see the pound signs in his eyes. This was a massive thing for me, I just didn't know what to do for the best. I was basically being made to choose between his dad, a new house, and all that went with that, and, on the other side, my kids. Not another impossible choice to be made. Jesus Christ, what was I supposed to do? I had to think about Owen, as well, and our standard of living, which was a struggle, I admit, though I couldn't justify leaving the North. We had no end of arguments about it, Paul wouldn't budge from his decision. We would do it. End of.

I was hoping that it would be quite a while before we needed to go, I put it at the back of my mind for now. When I told Angus that we would do it, he was really pleased, though he told me that it wouldn't be for a while as he was doing okay, even though he was falling all over the place and had fallen into the grandfather clock and smashed its face the other night. That didn't sound good to me. As I had no idea how to tell Tyler and Sarah, or the rest of the family I kept it to myself for a while. It was coming up to Christmas, we were all at Dina and Paddy's house, Harry was over. Mum and Dad were there and all the kids. It was a lovely day; we all had a good laugh and we played party games. Paul behaved himself until after he had a couple of beers, when he announced to everyone that we were thinking of moving to Somerset. No warning to me beforehand. He just blurted it out. I was really angry and speechless, what the hell was he thinking, it wasn't his place to announce that before I had a chance to talk to anyone. The kids just looked at me and asked me if it was true. My Mum looked upset and Dad, too. I just made light of it, saying that nothing had been decided yet, Angus had only recently asked us if we would go down and take care of him, if anything should happen to him. I reassured everybody that this was not something that was going to happen yet, I think I got away with it.

My Mum took me to one side to ask if I was sure about it. I told her I didn't have much of a choice, Paul was hell bent on doing it, he wanted to get the house and all that went with it. She was worried, she told me that my dad hadn't been too well. He had been complaining about a pain in his neck and he looked in pain. I noticed that he was a strange colour, and you could see the pain in his face. He kept wincing in pain. He told me that he thought he must have caught a nerve in his neck or something, it just wouldn't go away. He was clearly struggling and not doing very well at all. When we left to go home, I was livid with Paul for blurting the Somerset thing out without giving me the chance to talk to everyone first. He just told me I was overreacting, and they needed to be told. I was so cross I didn't speak all the way home. I was worried about my dad, too, something wasn't right there. My Mum said he was making a big deal out of it, as he had been moaning on about it for ages, she made light of it. She still hadn't forgiven Dad for having the affair and dragging us all to Hackness. She just couldn't seem to let that go.

Christmas Day came, we spent it at home with Owen. He was toddling around by then, and Evangeline and Ged came over with Yolanda. We had a lovely day; Evangeline and I cooked a meal. In the evening, we had a few drinks and played games. When the phone rang on Boxing Day, I wasn't prepared for what came next. Angus had collapsed, a neighbour had found him on the floor in the kitchen that morning. He had been there all night. He had fallen and banged his head. The neighbour called an ambulance, Angus had been taken to hospital, where they confirmed that he'd suffered a massive stroke. It transpired that he had been having a series of mini strokes over the last few months, which explained the falling in the garden, the bumping into things in the house. He had actually been worse than what he'd told us. Paul was manic.

I was in shock, I didn't know what to do, it was Boxing Day, I wasn't prepared for this. Paul started flapping around and I thought he was genuinely concerned about his dad. He started packing up the car, saying he would go and fill it up with petrol. I told him we should wait to see what the doctors say first, we didn't know the situation, we needed to think about it before we just jumped in the car and left. I told him that I had my job and the kids to think about, I couldn't just get in the car and go.

Paul just looked me in the eye and said, "we have to go today, right now. That bloody cleaner will move in the house and then we won't get it."

I couldn't believe my ears.

Paul was more bothered about the cleaner getting the house than his dad, which was absolutely ridiculous. He was panicking big time, he just kept saying we need to get ourselves down there to protect the inheritance, there's no way I am letting that bitch get everything. I had no choice; it was all such a rush. I couldn't think straight. I had to get Owen ready and agreed to drive down there with Paul straight away. What the hell would Tyler and Sarah think about me, I was being forced to make yet another impossible choice at their cost. I just had to go.

Lightning Source UK Ltd.
Milton Keynes UK
UKHW022100011221
394912UK00009B/434